Immigration—
The Beleaguered
Bureaucracy

MILTON D. MORRIS

Immigration— The Beleaguered Bureaucracy

THE BROOKINGS INSTITUTION
Washington, D.C.

Library of Congress Cataloging in Publication data:

Morris, Milton D.
  Immigration—the beleaguered bureaucracy.
  Includes bibliographical references and index.
    1. United States—Emigration and immigration—
Government policy. I. Title.
JV6493.M673 1984   325.73   84-22962
ISBN 0-8157-5838-3
ISBN 0-8157-5837-5 (pbk.)

9 8 7 6 5 4 3 2 1

THE BROOKINGS INSTITUTION is an independent organization devoted to nonpartisan research, education, and publication in economics, government, foreign policy, and the social sciences generally. Its principal purposes are to aid in the development of sound public policies and to promote public understanding of issues of national importance.

The Institution was founded on December 8, 1927, to merge the activities of the Institute for Government Research, founded in 1916, the Institute of Economics, founded in 1922, and the Robert Brookings Graduate School of Economics and Government, founded in 1924.

The Board of Trustees is responsible for the general administration of the Institution, while the immediate direction of the policies, program, and staff is vested in the President, assisted by an advisory committee of the officers and staff. The by-laws of the Institution state: "It is the function of the Trustees to make possible the conduct of scientific research, and publication, under the most favorable conditions, and to safeguard the independence of the research staff in the pursuit of their studies and in the publication of the results of such studies. It is not a part of their function to determine, control, or influence the conduct of particular investigations or the conclusions reached."

The President bears final responsibility for the decision to publish a manuscript as a Brookings book. In reaching his judgment on the competence, accuracy, and objectivity of each study, the President is advised by the director of the appropriate research program and weighs the views of a panel of expert outside readers who report to him in confidence on the quality of the work. Publication of a work signifies that it is deemed a competent treatment worthy of public consideration but does not imply endorsement of conclusions or recommendations.

The Institution maintains its position of neutrality on issues of public policy in order to safeguard the intellectual freedom of the staff. Hence interpretations or conclusions in Brookings publications should be understood to be solely those of the authors and should not be attributed to the Institution, to its trustees, officers, or other staff members, or to the organizations that support its research.

Foreword

IMMIGRATION has become an increasingly prominent national
issue during the past decade. The entry of large numbers of
refugees, many without prior approval, and dramatic increases
in illegal immigration have raised widespread concern about
how government treats those claiming refugee status, how it
handles the resettlement of refugees, and especially how it
might effectively curtail illegal immigration. These concerns
have prompted numerous studies and legislative efforts to
devise policies for better controlling immigration. The most
recent such effort was the Simpson-Mazzoli bill, which made
its way through both the House and the Senate before dying
in conference committee as the Ninety-eighth Congress adjourned.

In this study Milton D. Morris, a former senior fellow in the
Brookings Governmental Studies program, addresses many of
the concerns about controlling immigration by focusing on the
character and performance of the immigration bureaucracy—
primarily the Immigration and Naturalization Service and the
State Department's Bureau of Consular Affairs. He suggests
that many of the problems result from serious shortcomings
in the administration of immigration policies. He points out
that the immigration bureaucracy has long suffered from
inadequate funding, unclear objectives, and faulty structure
and procedures. These problems have become particularly

glaring during the past decade as the pressures for entry into the country have intensified. In view of Congress's great difficulty in enacting major policy reforms, some progress toward reducing illegal immigration might be achieved through improved performance of the immigration bureaucracy.

The author is grateful to the Edna McConnell Clark Foundation, the Rockefeller Brothers Fund, and the Revson Foundation for supporting the study; to Martha Derthick, Paul Peterson, James Sundquist, Albert Mayio, and the six anonymous reviewers of the manuscript for their thoughtful critiques of drafts of the study; to Roy Chatterjee, Andrew Linehan, Deborah Rose, and Carolyn Rutsch for their research assistance; to Diane Hodges, Julie Bailes, Pamela Harris, and Thomas Somuah for administrative and secretarial support; to Nancy Davidson and Venka Mcintyre for their editorial services; and to Diana Regenthal for indexing the book.

All the views expressed in this book are those of the author and should not be ascribed to the foundations that supported the project, or the trustees, officers, or staff of the Brookings Institution.

BRUCE K. MAC LAURY
President

October 1984
Washington, D.C.

Contents

1

Controlling Immigration: A Problem of Administration

ON June 20, 1984, the House of Representatives concluded an intense and sometimes dramatic seven-day debate by passing the Immigration Reform and Control Act of 1983, also known as the Simpson-Mazzoli bill.[1] The vote was an extremely close 216–211 in favor, with the outcome in doubt until the final seconds of the tally. The bill's weary, emotion-choked floor manager, Representative Romano L. Mazzoli, Democrat of Kentucky, seemed to reflect the feeling of the entire House as he expressed relief and gratitude that the House had finally acted after years of debate and delays.

Passage by the House was the most difficult and important step in an over a decade-long effort by the federal government to enact immigration reform aimed at reducing illegal immigration. There had been numerous studies by congressional committees, bills introduced in both chambers, studies by the executive branch, and an exhaustive study by a Select Commission on Immigration, all in an effort to deal with the rapidly growing problem of illegal immigration. The Simpson-Mazzoli bill was a product of these efforts, particularly those of the select commission, on which both Representative Mazzoli and

---

1. See *Congressional Record*, daily edition (June 20, 1984), pp. 6088–6185. On this date H.R. 1510 was incorporated into the Senate bill of the same name (S. 529).

the bill's Senate sponsor, Alan K. Simpson, Republican of Wyoming, had served. While the Senate had passed a version of the Simpson-Mazzoli bill first in 1982 and again in 1983, the House proved reluctant to act. In the final days of the turbulent lame-duck session of the Ninety-seventh Congress, it briefly debated and then shelved one version of the bill, claiming insufficient time to consider it. Again, in the first session of the Ninety-eighth Congress, several House committees considered the bill and proposed changes, but it languished in the Rules Committee, a victim of numerous disagreements among House members and fear by the House leadership about the political implications of acting on so controversial a bill with a presidential election on the horizon. It was therefore a major accomplishment when the bill passed the House on June 20, 1984.

But the House vote did not mean the delays were over. It appeared for a time that a conference committee would iron out the differences between the House and Senate versions, but the fragile compromise that had allowed the bill to squeak through the House began to collapse. Although most Democratic House members and the leadership had supported the bill, two of the three candidates for the Democratic party's presidential nomination expressed mild opposition, reflecting their own uncertainty about the political implications of either position in an election year. When the Democratic national convention convened just weeks after the House vote, Hispanic delegates demonstrated intense opposition to the bill. Democratic nominee Walter F. Mondale stiffened his opposition as well, and President Ronald Reagan, who had supported earlier efforts to pass the bill, suddenly found the House-passed version too expensive and withdrew his support, thereby drastically reducing its chances of becoming law. The bill's supporters worked hard to keep it alive, but as Congress adjourned for the summer, it seemed virtually certain that the bill was dead. However, when Congress reconvened after the summer recess the bill suddenly found a new life. House and Senate conferees worked feverishly to resolve the many conflicts over the House version. While they succeeded in settling most of them, a few key issues remained as stumbling blocks. Insufficient time and a lack of enthusiasm by most members of Congress for tackling the issue again resulted in the bill's demise when the Ninety-eighth Congress adjourned.

The closeness of the House vote and the subsequent collapse of support for the Simpson-Mazzoli bill are not surprising. The fact that the measure came so close to fruition in an election year is perhaps more surprising. Immigration policy has always been extremely controversial, reflecting at once the public's fears about the effects of immigration, deep commitment to the principle of an open country, and the special interests of many employers and ethnic groups to maintain liberal immigration. Even among those who have been convinced about the need for reform to increase the country's control over immigration, there have been widely divergent views about how this should be done.

The central issues in the past decade's debate about immigration and the ones tackled by the Simpson-Mazzoli bill are: how much immigration the country can prudently allow; what should be done to control illegal immigration; what should be done about the millions of illegal immigrants already residing here; and how the adjudication of immigration disputes and particularly asylum and refugee claims and claimants might be handled. The Senate version of the Simpson-Mazzoli bill addressed all of these issues.[2] It proposed an annual ceiling of 425,000 on immigrants, imposed penalties on employers who knowingly hire illegal immigrants, and provided for a phased extension of immigrant status to those in the country illegally before January 1980. The House deleted the cap on immigration and modified the provisions affecting employer penalties, legalization of illegal immigrants, and the treatment of refugee issues. In addition, the House acted to significantly strengthen the administration of immigration policy.

The lengthy deliberations on immigration issues in Congress

2. S. 529, Immigration Reform and Control Act of 1983.

heretofore have been conspicuously inattentive to the need for effective administration of immigration policy. The concern has almost always been how to devise new policies to deal with alleged problems. This inattention is especially noteworthy not only because the inadequacies in policy enforcement have been widely conceded for a long time, but because the policy reforms considered and adopted could be effective only with vastly improved administrative capability. In the deliberations on Simpson-Mazzoli, administration received substantial attention from both the Senate and House.

The Senate-approved version of Simpson-Mazzoli authorized a modest program of reciprocal waiver of the visitors' visa requirement for countries with very low visa refusal rates, changed the structure and procedure for some adjudication including refugee and asylum petitions, and declared the intention of Congress to authorize more funds for enforcement activities by the Immigration and Naturalization Service (INS). Section 111 of that bill declares:

> It is the sense of the Congress that an essential element of the program of immigration control and reform established by this Act is an increase in border patrol and other enforcement activities of the Immigration and Naturalization Service in order to prevent and deter the illegal entry of aliens to the United States.
>
> In order to do this in the most effective and efficient manner, it is the intent of the Congress to provide, through the annual authorization of appropriations process for the Department of Justice, for a controlled and closely monitored increase in the level of border patrol and of other appropriate enforcement activities of the Immigration and Naturalization Service to achieve an effective level of control of illegal immigration.

The House affirmed these Senate actions to strengthen enforcement of immigration policy and went somewhat further. For example, it authorized specific and substantial dollar increases in funds for enforcement activities by the INS and required the attorney general to submit plans for the new activities within two months after passage of the law. It also provided for expedited procedures for stopping and barring would-be illegal immigrants at the borders and created an adjudicative procedure including a new U.S. Immigration Board in the Justice Department. At the same time, the House seemed to go in the opposite direction by requiring INS investigators to obtain warrants to search open fields and farms for illegal immigrants, an action that would overturn a 6–3 Supreme Court decision to the contrary in *Oliver* v. *U.S.* and *Maine* v. *Thornton* and would probably increase the difficulty of apprehending illegal immigrants on farms.[3]

Although the net effect of these actions would be to improve the administration of immigration policy, the extent and character of that improvement is not clear. Perhaps more important, the congressional debate reflected a high degree of attention to and concern about a wide range of administrative arrangements aimed at protecting the civil rights of individuals.

Scope of the Study

This study is about the administration of immigration policy. It examines the evolution, character, and performance of the immigration bureaucracy in the context of the development of immigration policy. Analysts and public officials alike have been in agreement that there are serious flaws in the administration of immigration policy. However, there is considerable uncertainty about why this is so. Most analyses stress the inadequate funds available to the agencies responsible for enforcing immigration policy. The Senate version of the Simpson-Mazzoli bill reflected this view: it proposed to support increased appropriations but provided for very little structural or procedural reform. Even though the House version of that bill went somewhat further, its primary emphasis also was on increased funding.

Money clearly is the most important need of the immigration bureaucracy to finance much-needed expansion and improve-

3. 104 S.Ct. 1735 (1984).

ment in enforcement. However, there seem to be several other important problems as well—in the structure of the bureaucracy, enforcement procedures, and confusion over the objectives to be pursued by the immigration bureaucracy. Many of these factors are, in turn, the result of the country's deep and persistent ambivalence about immigration; the virtual inability of policymakers to satisfy the many conflicting demands with respect to immigration; and the failure of policymakers to recognize and respond to profound changes in the character of the enforcement task.

This study begins by reviewing the major forces that have influenced the development of U.S. immigration policy, particularly the country's ambivalence about immigration and the different approaches to immigration adopted by the executive and legislative branches. These factors and the political conflicts they engendered not only influenced the structure of the immigration bureaucracy and the approaches used in enforcing policy, but influenced public opinion about enforcement as well.

Next, the study reviews immigration trends and the forces behind them in order to clarify the changing demands on the immigration bureaucracy and the degree to which immigration really is susceptible to effective control through the approaches now available. Nothing has influenced the character of enforcement more than the rapidly increasing flow of aliens into this country. In evaluating the enforcement effort and measures to improve it, the current and anticipated pressures for entry must be considered.

Much of the debate about immigration reform rests on the assumption that the country is seriously threatened by an unprecedented surge in immigration and that steps must be taken immediately to prevent dire consequences for the country. The Senate version of the Simpson-Mazzoli bill, in fact, assumed this condition and responded to it by imposing a lid on all immigration. The evidence examined in chapter 3 suggests that while illegal immigration is widespread, may be damaging to the country, and needs to be promptly and effectively controlled, the country is not about to be engulfed by a great alien tide. The forces behind current immigration, it argues, are similar to those behind earlier waves of immigration, and even though the country is more mature now than at the beginning of this century when immigration was similarly high, it has not lost its capacity to absorb immigrants and to benefit from their presence.

Several recent developments now pose special administrative or enforcement challenges for the immigration bureaucracy. One is the very rapid increase in travel to this country by foreign nationals for a number of different reasons—tourism, study, immigration, business. Another is the high incidence of illegal entries, especially overland from nearby countries. Still another is the growing number of emergency entrants seeking refuge, many unexpectedly and without authorization. Perhaps the most important of the recent developments is the movement toward adoption of the Simpson-Mazzoli bill. Not only would the bill have imposed a number of major new responsibilities on the immigration bureaucracy, as several members of Congress noted during the House debates, the effectiveness of the law in reducing illegal immigration would have depended primarily on a dramatic improvement in the capability of the INS to prevent illegal entries.

Chapter 4 reviews the development and performance of the immigration bureaucracy, focusing on flow management, internal control and enforcement, and the provision of routine services. In this connection, it considers the performance of Congress and the executive in allocating the resources needed, the impact of unclear or inadequate immigration policies, the growing prominence of the federal courts in shaping enforcement practices, and the impact of the character of immigration as both a domestic and international phenomenon. All of these factors appear to have greatly influenced the administration of immigration policy historically and will continue to do so. Thus this segment of the study views the current performance of the immigration bureaucracy not as the result of specific failures on any single front but as the result of a combination of several powerful forces.

This view helps to account for the difficulty in arriving at a consensus among analysts or policymakers about what needs to be done to greatly improve the administration of immigration policy. It also suggests why the steps called for in the Simpson-Mazzoli bill, though important and constructive, are unlikely to go very far in enabling the immigration bureaucracy to gain and maintain effective control of immigration now and in the future. In chapter 5, the study identifies some measures that are essential to an effective enforcement effort and the prospects for their adoption.

In considering remedies for the immigration bureaucracy, the study assumes that effective control of immigration, rather than complete cessation of illegal immigration, is the plausible national objective. It also assumes that a high standard of performance of the service responsibilities of the bureaucracy is indispensable to the effective control that is sought. As in virtually all other areas of public policy, voluntary compliance with the law must be assumed to be the rule, with administrative actions aimed at encouraging and facilitating this compliance and discouraging noncompliance by posing a credible threat of unacceptably high cost to would-be noncompliers.

In carrying out these objectives, the immigration bureaucracy has the added responsibility of walking the tightrope between effective enforcement and observing the civil rights of everyone in this country—citizen and noncitizen alike. As the study shows, this latter responsibility, though not unique to the immigration bureaucracy, is especially challenging for it. One reason is the special character of the enforcement task, especially where it involves actions and decisions at the country's borders or about unauthorized entrants whose claims to residency here are at best murky. Although the courts have noted the special problems in enforcement here, it is still not clear to what extent standards applied in enforcing immigration policy should be allowed to differ from other domestic law enforcement standards. Meanwhile, the general concern with civil rights since the mid-1960s and the growing political activism of several previously uninvolved groups that feel particularly threatened by civil rights violations are likely to keep this a prominent issue before policymakers for some time.

Even if bold reforms were made in the administration of immigration policy, immigration would still be difficult to control. As this study shows, both the country's experience with immigration and the current situation point to the inescapable conclusion that immigration cannot be fully controlled even with a full array of promising administrative and policy changes. The power of the forces behind immigration and the openness of the society make full control unachievable. What can be achieved, however, is a level of control at which the chances of being detected are high enough to deter most would-be violators of immigration laws. Thus the public will be persuaded that the country's borders and its immigration laws are reasonably intact.

This line of reasoning leads to several strategies for improving the performance of the immigration bureaucracy. The question is, what are the prospects for their adoption? The passage of the Simpson-Mazzoli bill by both houses provided a hopeful sign. For example, Congress displayed an encouraging degree of interest in improving administration and a willingness to authorize substantially increased funds for doing so. It also approved some important procedural and structural changes to speed up and make more fair some aspects of enforcement. But these actions are the relatively easy, noncontroversial ones. At most, they constitute a promising first step. Little evidence of interest in more far-reaching reforms emerged from the congressional deliberations. Moreover, the real test of the government's willingness to finance the immigration bureaucracy is not expressions of intent to increase funding or even generous budget authorizations, but the appropriation of funds earmarked for meeting critical needs. This has not yet occurred to the extent needed to significantly improve the immigration bureaucracy's performance. Perhaps, as this study concludes, the only changes that can be hoped for are modest incremental improvements in administration, which would at least help the country to maintain the status quo.

Data

Despite the country's long-standing pride in its immigrant tradition and the mounting concern about immigration since the early 1970s, immigration problems remain poorly understood, particularly in the area of administration. One reason for this is that data essential for describing and evaluating immigration trends and the performance of the immigration bureaucracy are scarce and uneven. One difficulty is that the principal sources of data on immigration are the routine compilations by the INS and the State Department's Bureau of Consular Affairs. However, the data they gather are primarily for internal administrative purposes, are often flawed, and often become available years after they are gathered, thus making thorough up-to-date analyses very difficult, if not impossible. Furthermore, the same types of data reported by the different agencies dealing with immigration often do not agree, creating considerable confusion.

Another difficulty is that reliable data on illegal immigration and illegal immigrants are virtually nonexistent. The very nature of illegal immigration makes it almost impossible to gather data and allows self-serving or misleading guesses. Data on both legal and illegal immigration are used in this study with full recognition of their limitations. The data limitations notwithstanding, this study draws attention to some of the urgent questions for policymakers to consider, and it encourages the search for ways to improve the country's exercise of a basic sovereign right—that of controlling its borders.

2

In Search of an Immigration Policy

As Ellis Island, the Statue of Liberty, and expressions such as the "open door" and the "melting pot" have come to signify, U.S. society thinks of itself as a nation of immigrants. Underlying that notion is the belief that the individual has the right to emigrate, that within reasonable limits those who desire admission should be allowed to enter the country, and that those who are admitted will be absorbed into a racially and ethnically diverse society that will be made richer by their presence. The immigrant tradition has been a source of intense pride to Americans, and many in the country and abroad consider it a distinctive feature of the society. President John F. Kennedy, like several presidents before him, often referred to this tradition publicly, and it was the keynote of his July 1961 message to Congress urging refugee legislation:

> From the earliest days of our history, this land has been a refuge for the oppressed, and it is proper that we now, as descendants of refugees and immigrants, continue our long humanitarian tradition of helping those who are forced to flee to maintain their lives as individual, self-sufficient human beings in freedom, self-respect, dignity, and health.[1]

1. "Letter to the President of the Senate and to the Speaker of the House Proposing Reorganization and Reenactment of Refugee Aid Legislation, July 21, 1961," in *Public Papers of the Presidents: John F. Kennedy, 1961* (Government Printing Office, 1962), p. 528.

Somewhat similar sentiments were expressed by presidential candidate Ronald Reagan in a 1980 Labor Day address at Liberty State Park in New Jersey when he praised the millions of immigrants who entered the country at nearby Ellis Island: "I want more than anything I have ever wanted to have an Administration that will, through its actions, at home and in the international arena, let millions of people know that Miss Liberty still lifts her lamp beside the golden door."[2]

But there is also another side to the immigrant tradition that is evident from places like Krome North, the government's sometimes squalid detention center in Miami and one of several camps holding Haitian entrants or "boat people." These people risked their lives in fleeing their impoverished homeland in small creaky boats—perfect examples of the "wretched refuse" and the "huddled masses yearning to breathe free" whom poet Emma Lazarus's inscription on the base of the Statue of Liberty eloquently welcomed to this country. But U.S. officials refused to treat them as the refugees they claim that they are and have been seeking to expel them. Others, too, have met with harsh rejection in seeking entry. Nonwhites were virtually excluded for most of the country's history, and currently Salvadorans fleeing from the turmoil in their homeland are being denied refuge and face expulsion when apprehended.

Such treatment is in sharp contrast with the sentiments expressed by Presidents Kennedy and Reagan, but this contrast reflects a deep and long-standing ambivalence about immigration. While many people have been vigorous proponents of a liberal or open door approach to immigration, others have been fearful of its likely adverse social, economic, and political effects on the country. These conflicting views have been present in the same individual. One example is James Madison, who welcomed immigration, noting that "that part of America which has encouraged them [immigrants] most, has advanced most

2. Quoted in Larry Fuchs, "The Current Policy Debate on Illegal Immigration," paper prepared for the Wingspread Workshop on Labor Market Impacts of Immigration, August 8, 1982, p. 8.

rapidly in agriculture, population, and the arts," but also worried that immigrant groups often clung to their language and culture, thereby contributing to cultural fragmentation.[3] Even as the young national government sought to encourage immigration and several states sought to attract them as settlers, many people echoed Madison's fear, noting that immigration might threaten national homogeneity, undermine democratic values and institutions, and dilute the quality of the country's racial stock.

The country's ambivalence about immigration intensified as the level of immigration began to rise sharply after 1840. Not only did concern grow about broad effects on the society, but many people became concerned about the financial burden that immigrants sometimes imposed on the localities where they settled. Moreover, workers and their representatives began to blame immigrants for reducing their job opportunities and interfering with their efforts to organize.

In spite of these misgivings, the country needed the immigrants to expedite conquest of the frontier by settling and cultivating the land, helping to construct a transportation system that would link the interior to the budding urban centers and coastal markets, and providing labor for the mines and burgeoning industrial centers. By the early 1880s, the fears and hostilities toward immigrants became powerful enough to produce strong pressures for restrictive legislation. The conquest of the West was nearing completion, there was increasing competition for jobs, and the country was becoming less confident about the prospects for future growth. In the view of historian John Higham, the period between 1885 and 1897 was "one of recurring calamities and almost unrelieved discontent culminating in the savage depression of 1893–97."[4]

Starting in 1882, Congress enacted laws imposing qualitative

3. Quoted in William S. Bernard, *American Immigration Policy: A Reappraisal* (Harper Brothers, 1950), p. 61.
4. John Higham, *Strangers in the Land: Patterns of American Nativism 1860-1925* (Atheneum, 1975), p. 68.

restrictions on immigration and suspending (and later abolishing) Chinese immigration. These laws were but a half-hearted attempt at restricting immigration, however. Except for Chinese immigration, which came to a virtual halt, immigration continued unchecked, reaching a peak of 1.2 million in 1907 and averaging nearly 1 million annually for the decade between 1901 and 1910. Bills to reduce immigration continued to be debated in Congress frequently, but only in 1917 was one weak measure—a literacy requirement for immigrants—enacted after four presidential vetoes. Four years later, Congress adopted a temporary law imposing stringent numerical limits on immigration based on the national origins of the population. These were made permanent and even more rigid in 1924.

Factors in the Policy Transition

The transition from an open door policy to a highly restrictive one was the result of not only domestic economic problems, but an upsurge in nationalism, growing anti-Catholic sentiment, spreading pseudoscientific racism and cultural chauvinism, and a growing fear that outbreaks of political turmoil abroad might be brought to this country by immigrants. The mix of these many forces shaped the gradual evolution of immigration policies and their enforcement. Furthermore, sharp differences between the executive branch and Congress helped shape policy development. While Congress invariably stressed domestic concerns relating to immigration policy and so tended to support restrictive policies, presidents tended to take a broad global view of immigration and to encourage liberal policies. A review of these factors and public attitudes toward immigration can lead to a better understanding of the current problems in shaping immigration policy and in implementing these policies.

Concerns about the Labor Market

Undoubtedly one of the most powerful forces to affect immigration policy has been the fear that immigrants will displace domestic workers, depress wages, and contribute to poor working conditions. That fear arose early in the country's history (it lay behind the scattered anti-immigration riots of the middle and late nineteenth century and the strong nativist sentiments of that time) and has increasingly influenced the character of immigration policy since then. In fact, much of the political debate over immigration policy in recent years has revolved around the labor market issue. Organized labor has sought to restrict the level of immigration and then to secure special legislative protections for the domestic worker beyond the limits already imposed. In this regard it won the inclusion of a labor certification requirement in the McCarran-Walter Act of 1952, the country's basic immigration law, and a slightly strengthened version in the Immigration and Nationality Act of 1965.

Section 212(a)(14) of the McCarran-Walter Act invested the secretary of labor with the authority to exclude an alien worker seeking admission to the country if the secretary determined that the locality of the alien's destination had sufficient workers willing and able to do the work that the alien would be admitted to do. In its report on the bill, the House Judiciary Committee noted that

> this provision will adequately provide for the protection of American labor against an influx of aliens entering the U.S. for the purpose of performing skilled or unskilled labor where the economy of individual localities is not capable of absorbing them at the time they desire to enter this country.[5]

A strengthened labor certification provision was adopted in the 1965 law, but like the 1952 provision, it has had only a modest effect on the entry of workers. Labor's more important

5. *Revising the Laws Relating to Immigration, Naturalization, and Nationality,* H. Rept. 1365, 82 Cong. 2 sess. (GPO, 1952), p.51.

victories have come in shifting the official emphasis in immigration policy away from labor force augmentation to those of
family reunification and refugee resettlement, and in containing
the use of temporary foreign workers.

These provisions eased the fears of organized labor somewhat, but concerns about continued use of temporary seasonal
workers and the sharp rise in illegal immigration during the
1970s have rekindled labor's fear of extensive job losses. Indeed,
the decade-long effort to legislate immigration reform that
would curtail illegal immigration has been motivated to a great
extent by the belief that illegal immigrants displace domestic
workers, depress wages, and contribute to poor working
conditions.

It is unclear how serious a problem these alleged adverse
effects are; and the extent to which concern about them should
influence immigration policy generally, and responses to illegal
immigration in particular, is the subject of major disagreements
among analysts and policymakers. Part of the problem is that
the effects of immigrants on the labor market are complex and
may be interpreted in several ways. Macroeconomic theorists
claim that the labor market is highly elastic and that new job
opportunities arise as consumption increases in response to
the rising population resulting from immigration. Therefore,
in their view immigrants improve the economy instead of
hurting it. Furthermore, some analysts note, immigrants have
always been needed to hold low-wage, low-prestige jobs that
domestic workers are reluctant to take, and therefore they are
usually not direct competitors with most domestic workers.
Other analysts tend to see a much greater likelihood that
immigrants compete with and displace domestic workers. To
support this view they point to the relatively high rates of
unemployment that coincide with the increased immigration
of the past decade and to anecdotal evidence from particular
localities or occupations. In urging immigration reform, INS
officials also have persistently emphasized the adverse effects
of illegal immigration on the labor market. They have even

described some recent drives to expel illegal immigrants as job-creating efforts.

Part of the reason for the differing views about the labor market effects of immigration is that the effects vary for different segments of the labor market and for different types of labor markets. There is some evidence, for example, that the jobs of unskilled, low-wage domestic workers are more likely to be threatened than those of highly educated or skilled workers. Farmers in the West and Southwest find legal and illegal immigrants an immensely valuable addition to the labor force—in many cases they make up the entire seasonal agricultural labor force. The same is true for hotels, restaurants, and other service facilities in urban areas. At the same time, the domestic labor force in these areas will almost certainly be hurt by the direct competition for jobs and the lower wage levels that usually prevail when large numbers of immigrant workers are present.

Another source of differing views might be the condition of the economy at the time the evidence is examined. Immigrants seem likely to be less of a threat to domestic workers when the economy is vibrant and growing than when it is sluggish and declining. For this reason, those who consider the effects question in the context of the past few years of a weak economy and high unemployment are likely to reach a different conclusion from those who consider it over a longer time period.

Racial and Ethnic Prejudice

No group of immigrants to the United States has ever escaped the prejudice of those who arrived before them. By the mid-1850s that prejudice fueled much of the hostility toward immigrants. Initially, the anti-immigrant sentiment was directed mainly at the Chinese and Japanese, particularly those concentrated in large numbers in the West. Racial and ethnic prejudice and the fear of declining employment opportunities combined to foster measures to restrict Japanese and Chinese immigrants: in 1879 California enacted a series of discriminatory laws against Chinese and Japanese immigrants; in 1882 Congress enacted laws suspending Chinese immigration; and in 1907, faced with the likely adoption of anti-Japanese legislation, President Theodore Roosevelt negotiated an agreement with Japan under which it voluntarily prevented Japanese immigration. By 1910 nationals of virtually all Asian countries were excluded from the country as immigrants.

A strong prejudice also developed against the southern and eastern European immigrants who were entering the country in large numbers by the 1870s. In the face of a dramatic increase in immigration from these countries at the turn of the century, policymakers began to seek ways to curtail that flow in favor of nationals of northern and western Europe, who were of similar racial and cultural background to the majority of the white population. The search for discriminatory measures was initially justified by crude assertions of the racial and cultural inferiority of the unwanted immigrant groups. However, by the 1890s a large body of pseudoscientific writings began to appear purporting to document the racial inferiority of non-Anglo-Saxons and the potential dangers they posed to American society.

This pseudoscientific assault on the open door policy began in earnest in 1890 with a series of articles by Superintendent of the Census Francis A. Walker, who complained in an address to the American Economic Association that the new immigrants were drawn from "great stagnant pools of population which no current of intellectual or moral activity has stirred for ages."[6] Following Walker, other otherwise distinguished intellectuals sought to establish the Teutonic origins of U.S. political institutions and to suggest that these institutions were endangered by the admission of inferior races like the Slavs and Latins.

Racial and cultural factors were also emphasized by the Dillingham Commission (headed by Senator William P. Dil-

6. Francis A. Walker, "The Tide of Economic Thought," in *Publications of the American Economic Association*, vol. 6 (1891), p. 37.

lingham, Republican of Vermont), which had been established by Congress in 1907 to study immigration.[7] Its report purported to show that some ethnic groups tended to be more difficult to assimilate than others and so were less desirable as immigrants, advocated steps to reduce the influx of such groups, and stressed that racial and ethnic characteristics of immigrants were among the critical factors to affect society. The report's suggestion that immigration indeed had widespread adverse effects on the country and that immigrants tended to cluster in overcrowded urban ghettos and to be overrepresented in mental hospitals lent considerable respectability to the pseudo-scientific assertions about the racial and ethnic inferiority of the immigrant stream from southern and eastern Europe. The commission's report was well received in Congress and aided the enactment of the literacy requirement for immigrants in 1917 (over President Woodrow Wilson's veto) and the quota law of 1921, known as the Johnson Act.

The influence of racial and ethnic prejudice on immigration policy was further strengthened by a report prepared by eugenicist Harry H. Laughlin for the House Committee on Immigration and Naturalization in 1922. According to Laughlin, scientific evidence showed that all foreigners were inferior, especially those from southern and eastern Europe. He therefore concluded that "the surest biological principle to direct the future of America along safe and sound racial channels is to control the hereditary quality of the immigration stream."[8] Supported by these conclusions, Congress moved in 1924 to tighten and make permanent the 1921 quota law and the preference system based on national origins.

The 1924 law, like its predecessor of 1921, calculated each country's immigrant quota on the basis of the "national origins principle." That is, the quota for any given country was to be a specified percentage of its nationals residing in the United

7. *Reports of the Immigration Commission*, 41 vols. (GPO, 1911).

8. *Analysis of America's Modern Melting Pot*, Hearings before the House Committee on Immigration and Naturalization, 67 Cong. 3 sess. (GPO, 1923), pp. 725–831.

States at a specified time. The 1921 law had provided that each country's quota would be limited to 3 percent of the population of its nationals residing in the United States in 1910, and on this basis it had established an overall ceiling of 356,000 immigrants per year. Accordingly, heavy immigration from the northern and western European countries was permitted, whereas the flow from southern and eastern Europe was curtailed. The 1924 immigration law retained this principle, but reduced each country's quota to 2 percent of the population of its nationals in the United States in 1890. The overall ceiling was thus reduced to a mere 154,000 immigrants a year. Self-governing Western Hemisphere countries were exempt from these ceilings and so immigrants from these countries were not included in the quotas.

By the end of World War II, the influence of racial and ethnic prejudice on immigration policy began to diminish as a result of several developments at home and abroad. For one thing, the wartime alliance between the United States and China led to the repeal in 1943 of the Chinese exclusion laws that China so deeply resented. Three years later, the newly independent India and the Philippines were assigned immigration quotas for the first time and thus the exclusion of their nationals was ended. Moreover, establishment of communist regimes in eastern Europe and political unrest in some southern European countries immediately after the war prompted the United States to admit large numbers of Europeans earlier regarded as inferior. Meanwhile, on the domestic scene the character of racial and ethnic discrimination was changing to a predominantly black-white configuration. The same Europeans whose presence had been vigorously opposed earlier now had considerable political strength and could influence immigration policies.

As the country attempted a comprehensive review of its immigration policies after the war, the discriminatory character of these policies became increasingly controversial. Although the hostility to Latin and Slavic immigrants from Europe had all but disappeared, Asian and African peoples were still excluded under the national origins principle. What to do about that principle became a central policy issue in the two decades following the war. The United States now had a position of leadership in the world and a growing desire to shed so prominent a symbol of American racism as the national origins principle. All the same, the strict numerical ceiling based on this principle was retained by Congress in the McCarran-Walter Act of 1952 over a veto of the bill by President Harry S. Truman.

Debate about discriminatory immigration policy did not subside after 1952. If anything, it grew more heated as the rapidly changing international community in which the United States sought to assert moral and political leadership exerted its own enormous pressure for change. Moreover, by the early 1960s a large segment of U.S. society joined in a massive civil rights movement to end racial discrimination in public policy. At the peak of the civil rights revolution, a year after the enactment of the sweeping Civil Rights Act of 1964 and just before passage of the historic Voting Rights Act, Congress ushered in a new era in immigration policy by enacting the Immigration and Nationality Act of 1965. That law abandoned the national origins system, and with it race and ethnicity as considerations in granting access to the country. It established an annual ceiling of 170,000 immigrants from the Eastern Hemisphere, with each country in the hemisphere entitled to a maximum of 20,000; and for the first time a ceiling was imposed on the Western Hemisphere, of 120,000, so that the total annual ceiling was 290,000.

With these changes the 1965 law brought immigration policy in line with changing national attitudes toward race and ethnicity and with the new international order in which many new non-European states were demanding to be treated as equals.

National Security Jitters

The possibility that immigrants might endanger national security has been another source of great concern. This fear of subversion, which has been more prominent at some times than at others, has been around since the United States was newly formed. As John Higham has pointed out, "From the 1790s a fear of foreign radicals had lurked in the corners of the American mind."[9] Indeed, it had prompted enactment of the Alien and Sedition Laws in 1798. It was a particularly strong force during and immediately after World War I because many Americans at that time saw Europe as a cauldron of radical socialism and revolutionary politics. The overthrow of the Czarist regime in Russia in 1917 had emboldened revolutionaries and heightened political tensions throughout the continent, and the resulting uneasiness quickly reached the United States. Many public officials here feared that immigrants would spread this revolutionary spirit to this country and urged that firm restrictions be applied. This fear intensified when elements of U.S. labor began to show signs of increasing restiveness and the residences of some public officials were bombed, including that of Commissioner of Immigration Frederick Howe, whose house was hit in 1919.

Largely in response to the growing fear of subversion from radicals, the secretaries of state and labor in 1918 ordered that a visa requirement be introduced so that individuals migrating to the United States could be screened before embarking for this country. This visa requirement was later enacted into law. Within the country, the Immigration Commission—the forerunner of what is now the Immigration and Naturalization Service—used its sweeping power to conduct surveillance of and raids on aliens suspected of subversive ties.

Not surprisingly, in this atmosphere, the 1921 immigration law imposing strict numerical ceilings and promising to provide for admission of a larger proportion of the "right kind" of immigrants was easily enacted. Yet there was substantial opposition to the drastic curtailment proposed as well as to the arbitrary treatment that many aliens in the country would

9. Higham, *Strangers in the Land,* p. 7

receive under this law. Opponents argued that the times required the United States to respond generously to the plight of the Europeans, and that famine and radicalism might engulf the entire European continent if it failed to do so.

National security concerns subsided somewhat with the introduction of the visa requirement and enactment of the quota laws, but they sprang up again during and after World War II with the growing fear of communist subversion. At the same time that the country was preparing to admit thousands of Europe's displaced persons, the anticommunist crusade of Senator Joseph McCarthy was gathering steam. Not surprisingly, immigrants were viewed by some with suspicion. The 1953 INS annual report, for example, complained that among the alien groups were "some who are notorious rather than noteworthy, and whose deeds are full of malicious intent rather than of contributions to democratic ideals."[10]

Although considerably less consuming in recent years, this fear of subversion has continued to influence immigration policy and its administration. Current immigration law still excludes individuals who have been affiliated with groups judged to be sympathetic to communism or other revolutionary ideologies, and the same concern influences the processing of refugees.

Public Attitudes about the Open Door

A number of U.S. presidents have assumed that the public strongly favors liberal immigration. President Woodrow Wilson, for example, invoked what he perceived as the public's support for the open door tradition in his 1915 veto of the bill imposing a literacy requirement on immigrants:

> If the people of this country have made up their minds to limit the number of immigrants by arbitrary tests and so reverse the policy of all the generations of Americans that have gone before

10. Immigration and Naturalization Service, *Annual Report, 1953*, p. 2.

them, it is their right to do so. I am their servant and have no
license to stand in their way. But I do not believe that they
have.[11]

Yet there is no firm evidence that the public has ever enthu-
siastically shared this sentiment. On the contrary, public attention to immigrants and to immigration policy seems to have
been very limited, sporadic, and confined mainly to local or
regional concerns. Only small segments of the population seem
to have shown any great interest in immigration policy at any
particular time, and most have remained largely indifferent
even though immigration issues have been hotly debated almost
continuously at the national level since 1945. Moreover, public
opinion surveys since 1946 reveal a remarkably consistent lack
of enthusiasm for extensive immigration and suggest much
less general commitment to the open door tradition than public
officials have assumed.

Four Gallup surveys between 1946 and 1977 (table 2-1) reveal
that the public has been overwhelmingly and consistently
opposed to increased immigration. No more than 8 percent of
the respondents in any year favored increased immigration,
and in all the years polled except for 1965 more respondents
favored reduced immigration than the existing level—hardly a
ringing endorsement of the open door tradition. The stability
of these attitudes over this period of time is especially remarkable since the question "Do you believe that immigration should
be increased, decreased, or kept at current levels?" was asked
at times when developments were contributing to major changes
in immigration.

In 1946, for example, the country was preparing to admit
the first of the postwar European refugees. In 1965 years of
bitter debate culminated in the adoption of a new immigration
law that abolished the national origins principle and revised
the ceiling on immigration, and President Lyndon B. Johnson

11. Message of President Woodrow Wilson to the Senate, *Congressional Record*
(January 28, 1915), pp. 2481–82.

Table 2-1. *Public Attitudes toward Change in Level of Immigration, 1946–77*

| Poll year | Attitude toward immigration | | |
	Should be increased	Should be decreased	Should remain unchanged
1946[a]	5	51	32
1965	8	33	39
1976	5	52	37
1977	7	42	37

Sources: George H. Gallup, *The Gallup Poll, Public Opinion, 1935–1971*, vol. 1 (Random House, 1972), p. 555; *The Gallup Poll: Public Opinion, 1935–1971*, vol. 3, pp. 1952–53; "The Gallup Study of Attitudes Toward Illegal Aliens, Conducted for the Immigration and Naturalization Service" (Princeton: Gallup Organization, 1976), p. 10; *The Gallup Poll: Public Opinion, 1972–77*, vol. 2 (Wilmington, Del.: Scholarly Resources, 1978), p. 1050.
a. Refers to European immigrants only.

offered to admit as refugees all who wanted to leave Cuba. And in 1976 and 1977 the Indochinese refugees were beginning to arrive in large numbers and thousands more were taking to the South China Sea in unseaworthy boats or were pouring overland into Thailand in flight from newly installed communist regimes.

More recent polls suggest that by 1980 the public clearly opposed the expanding levels of immigration. In a 1980 Roper survey (table 2-2), 80 percent of the respondents agreed that the number of legal immigrants admitted annually should be reduced, 91 percent supported an all-out effort to stop illegal immigration, and 63 percent wanted fewer Cuban refugees admitted.

Two features of current public attitudes toward immigration seem especially noteworthy. One is that public opposition to increased immigration is particularly strong with respect to illegal immigration. The other is that usually attitudes toward immigration do not vary greatly across economic or racial lines, even though differences are apparent. The low-income population tends to support reduced immigration and focus on the ill effects of immigrants on the country somewhat more than the high-income population. And although slightly more blacks

Table 2-2. Public Attitudes toward Immigration and Population Growth Issues, by Income and Race, June 1980
Percent

Issue	Agree						Disagree						Not sure
	Total	Income[a] High	Medium	Low	Race Black	White	Total	Income[a] High	Medium	Low	Race Black	White	
Make an all-out effort to stop illegal immigration	91	92	91	92	88	92	5	5	6	4	7	5	...
Reduce the number of legal immigrants admitted annually	80	75	80	81	82	80	16	21	15	14	12	16	5
Do nothing to slow population growth	20	17	19	20	33	18	73	78	75	73	56	75	7
Admit fewer Cuban refugees	63	60	61	66	60	64	...	35	36	30	35	33	...
Cuban refugees will turn out to be a bad thing	57	52	52	62	67	56	11	17	13	7	6	12	32

Source: Roper Reports, 80-6 (New York: Roper Organization, 1980).
a. High, medium, and low income defined respectively as $25,000 and above, $15,000–$25,000, and $7,000–$15,000.

than whites support reduced legal immigration or are pessimistic about the effects of immigrants, fewer blacks support immediate actions to curb illegal immigration.

Pressure Groups and Immigration Policy

As in many other areas of public policy, the attitudes of the general public have been less influential in shaping immigration policy than those of a much smaller segment of the population consisting of activists operating in pressure groups. Throughout much of the country's history, certainly during this century, interest groups have been powerful and decisive forces in determining U.S. immigration policy. Some of these groups (like the influential Immigration Restriction League, founded in 1894) disappeared by 1924, after numerical restrictions had been firmly established. Others survived and to this day pursue the same policies they started out with. Still other pressure groups remain active but have drastically changed their views about immigration over the years. Finally, the large-scale refugee admissions and increased attention to population growth and environmental issues in recent years have given rise to several new groups seeking to influence immigration policy.

Pressure groups have concentrated on a variety of different immigration issues, making it very difficult to compare them in terms of any specific issue. For example, some groups have confined themselves to the basic question of whether immigration policy should be more or less restrictive while others have been extensively involved in a number of detailed questions about what types of immigrants should be admitted or how government should go about curtailing illegal immigration. In discussing these groups, I will for convenience describe them in terms of whether they are opponents or proponents of expanded immigration.

The pressure groups that have been the most prominent opponents of expanded immigration over the past century fall into three broad categories: patriotic-nationalistic organizations such as the major veterans' groups, the Allied Patriotic Societies, Daughters of the American Revolution, and the Liberty Lobby; labor organizations such as the American Federation of Labor (AFL) before its merger with the Congress of Industrial Organizations (CIO); and the recently formed growth limitation organizations such as Zero Population Growth (ZPG) and the Federation for American Immigration Reform (FAIR).

Despite the diversity of their interests (some of which have changed over time), together these groups have articulated the many fears and prejudices that have helped to shape immigration policies in the United States. The patriotic-nationalistic groups have opposed liberal immigration policies, they claim, in order to protect the U.S. government and other institutions from people who do not understand them and might undermine them; they have also sought to keep out racially or culturally undesirable immigrants.[12] With the enactment of the 1965 immigration law, these ideas were emphatically rejected and have by and large disappeared from the major public debates about immigration policy.

The newer growth limitation organizations recoil from the ethnic and cultural chauvinism of the patriotic-nationalist groups but nevertheless argue that curbs should be put on immigration because it can have adverse effects on society and the environment. The philosophy of this group was summed up by John H. Tanton (chairman of ZPG's Immigration Study Committee) in the 1975 congressional hearings on the demographic effects of immigration: "Since immigration can significantly affect population growth, an immigration policy must be integrated into any such population stabilization policy." Noting that from a base of 220 million in 1975, immigration alone would add about 56 million to the country's projected population of 258 million by the year 2000, Tanton suggested that "it is probably through illegal immigration that the citizens of de-

12. *Restriction of Immigration,* Hearings before the House Committee on Immigration and Naturalization, 68 Cong. 1 sess. (GPO, 1925), p. 973.

veloped countries are most directly going to experience the population growth of the less developed countries."[13] These concerns have led ZPG to oppose increased legal immigration and to advocate actions to end illegal immigration. A somewhat similar position has been taken by FAIR, the newest of the major opponents of liberal immigration, except that it emphasizes a much broader array of likely adverse effects.

More and more long-time opponents of expanded immigration have come to adopt the arguments of ZPG and FAIR emphasizing the dangers of growth. In particular they argue that the economic reverses the United States has experienced since the mid-1970s and the intensifying pressure on governments to cope with the rapidly rising costs for basic services show that the country is unable to afford large numbers of immigrants.

On the side of expanded or liberal immigration policies is a set of similarly diverse interest groups: numerous ethnic groups representing the major ethnic segments of the country's population; liberal religious organizations, some of which have worked with immigrants for many years; liberal and progressive political and human rights organizations such as the American Civil Liberties Union and Americans for Democratic Action; and some labor and business organizations such as the AFL-CIO and the National Association of Manufacturers. These groups have been united in their support of expanded immigration policies but they have differed in the reasons for this support.

The ethnic groups clearly perceive themselves as beneficiaries of laws that promote immigration and they have sought to preserve the same benefits for their fellow nationals who might wish to immigrate. Moreover, most ethnic groups in the country have remained attentive to developments in their former homelands and they are among the first to urge a generous

13. *Illegal Aliens,* Hearings before the Subcommittee on Immigration, Citizenship, and International Law of the House Committee on the Judiciary, 94 Cong. 1 sess. (GPO, 1975), pp. 271–72.

response by the United States when political turmoil or economic distress causes people to flee. The Polish American Congress, American Jewish Council, Chinese Welfare Council, Italian-American Council, Mexican-American Legal Defense and Education Fund (MALDEF), and League of United Latin American Citizens (LULAC) are only a few of the ethnic groups that have been and remain vigorous advocates of expanded immigration. In recent years LULAC and MALDEF, with some other Hispanic organizations, have emerged as prominent and influential advocates of expanded immigration, especially now that most immigrants to the United States are Spanish-speaking and that attention has become focused on the high incidence of illegal entries by Mexicans.

Blacks are the newest segment of the population to take a special interest in the development of immigration policy. Blacks are not a recent immigrant group like the major ethnic groups and have displayed little interest in this issue until recently, even though there is considerable evidence that the group has been adversely affected by immigration more than almost any other major segment of U.S. society. Three developments combined to stimulate its recent interest in immigration policy: the great influx of refugees from Indochina after 1976 and the perception that these newcomers were actual or potential competitors for jobs, housing, and various forms of public assistance; the arrival of thousands of Haitian boat people and the federal government's harsh treatment of them, which raised to prominence the issue of racially discriminatory refugee policies; and the greater involvement of blacks in national politics in general and the simultaneous increase in their emphasis on cooperation with Hispanics in the political arena.

In the deliberations on the Simpson-Mazzoli bill, blacks emphasized in testimony before the Immigration Subcommittee their interest in the eradication of racially discriminatory refugee policies, protection of the civil rights of all foreign-born Americans and other ethnic minorities, and the improvement of existing processes for adjudicating immigration matters. At least at the national level, they have sidestepped the thorny questions about the effects of illegal immigration on the black population.

Business groups, particularly manufacturers and growers, have generally supported expanded immigration policies because they believe such policies help to strengthen the work force, whereas restrictive or discriminatory policies create risks to foreign trade. These groups have viewed immigration issues in terms of their effect on the free flow of production and exchange and have stressed the country's continuing need for immigrants to supplement the work force and help meet the demand for goods and services. At the same time, growers from the northeastern and southern United States have complained of shortages in agricultural labor and noted that these shortages could be relieved by immigration.[14]

Organized labor, one of the strongest and most active of the immigration lobby groups, has been both for and against liberal immigration. It was an early advocate of severe restrictions on immigration even though many of its members were immigrants. The AFL supported the literacy test law, the quota law, proposals for a temporary freeze on immigration in 1922, retention of Chinese exclusion, and the McCarran-Walter Act. However, other labor organizations, most notably the CIO, supported liberal immigration, as a CIO representative testifying before the Truman Commission on Immigration in 1951 asserted:

> The CIO realizes from past experience that immigration is automatically checked in periods of unemployment while it rises in periods of prosperity; that in the past, immigrants have contributed in innumerable ways to the wealth and well-being of this country . . . that new blood in industry, agriculture, business, and the professions enriches our national life; and that the best and most enlightened thought on this subject opposes

14. *Selective Immigration Legislation*, Hearings before the Immigration and Naturalization Committee, 68 Cong. 1 sess. (GPO, 1924), pp. 164, 209.

arbitrary, prejudiced, and superficial legislation to curb immigration into the United States.[15]

When the CIO and AFL merged, the CIO's position prevailed as the new AFL-CIO decided to support expanded immigration while attempting to ensure that domestic workers were given certain protections. Despite intolerably high unemployment, it supported the 1980 Refugee Act because, according to a representative of the AFL-CIO, the organization believes in "fundamental American values, values which place a premium on human life and freedom."[16] In the continuing debate about immigration policy, organized labor remains a vigorous opponent of temporary worker programs and favors strong measures to curtail illegal immigration, but it also supports a generally liberal immigration policy.

Several social and religious groups advocate liberal immigration policies, partly in response to the large number of refugees being admitted and the country's practice of relying on private voluntary agencies to resettle refugees. Even states and localities have become prominent lobbyists, especially on issues such as refugee admissions, the legalization of illegal immigrants, and the cost of the public service benefits they are believed to consume. The primary concern for local governments has been the growing cost of providing essential services and other support to refugees who are not yet self-sufficient and to illegal immigrants. In many localities this issue has become important enough to generate considerable interest in the formulation of immigration policy.

Because immigration is important to most major source countries, some have sought to influence U.S. immigration policies as well. By and large they have lobbied discreetly, expressing their concern to the State Department. But some have acted more directly, by appealing to members of Congress.

15. *Hearings before the U.S. President's Commission on Immigration and Naturalization*, Committee Print, House Committee on the Judiciary, 82 Cong. 1 sess. (GPO, 1952), p. 1622.

16. *Congressional Record*, daily edition (April 23, 1979), p. E1721.

Madame Chiang Kai-shek of China, for example, met with congressional leaders as part of a tour of the United States in 1943 to advocate repeal of the Chinese exclusion laws. The country with the greatest influence on U.S. immigration policy-making in recent years has been Mexico. Not only has it been a party to often protracted and acrimonious negotiations over illegal immigration and the bracero program (which admitted temporary farm workers), but Mexico has also loomed large in the making and implementation of U.S. immigration policies. The central immigration issue here—and a continuous source of tension—has been illegal immigration. Mexico has emphasized the binational character of the issue and the need for agreement between the two countries on policies that will stem the massive flow of Mexicans crossing the southern border illegally but will not deny Mexicans legal employment in this country. Specifically, Mexico insists that U.S. immigration policy should recognize and respond to the complex economic problems that push Mexicans into this country. Although Mexican authorities have not intervened directly in the deliberations on immigration policy in Congress, the knowledge that Mexico is apprehensive about any significant curtailment of access by its nationals to this country has been a major deterrent to strong legislative or administrative action to curb illegal immigration. Moreover, the issue has been discussed at virtually every meeting of the presidents of the two countries since 1972.

Congress and the President: Domestic versus International Interests

Probably no other major area of public policy has been the cause of as much conflict between Congress and the executive branch as immigration. Between 1882 and 1952 ten immigration laws were vetoed by six presidents with widely differing styles, perceptions of executive-legislative authority, and attitudes about the use of the veto power. One prime example of this conflict is the disagreement over the literacy requirement.

On May 21, 1896, the House of Representatives passed an immigration bill with a literacy requirement by a vote of 195–26. The same bill was approved by the Senate on December 17 of that year by the equally lopsided margin of 52–10. However, on March 2 of the following year outgoing President Grover Cleveland vetoed the bill, calling it a departure from the traditional American policy and declaring that it was out of harmony with the spirit of U.S. institutions.[17] Almost seventeen years later both houses of Congress again passed virtually identical legislation by similarly large majorities only to have it vetoed for the fourth time, this time by President Wilson, who complained that the bill would close the gates of asylum that had always been open and would "exclude those to whom the opportunities of elementary education have been denied without regard to their character, their purpose, or their natural capacity."[18] Congress prevailed two years later by enacting the legislation over President Wilson's veto.

Presidential vetoes notwithstanding, Congress remained the dominant force in shaping the country's immigration policies and took the initiative in formulating immigration policy for most of the past one hundred years. In December 1889 the two chambers of Congress established committees on immigration and proceeded to hold hearings on immigration policy. In one form or another the issue has remained on the congressional agenda since that time. Congress has debated immigration issues, commissioned studies, and developed legislation while the executive branch has tried, by and large unsuccessfully, to restrain the excesses of the Congress or to influence specific aspects of proposed actions. Congressional dominance diminished somewhat after World War II, however, with

---

17. Lawrence H. Chamberlain, *The President, Congress and Legislation* (Columbia University Press, 1946), p. 357.
18. *Congressional Record* (January 28, 1915), p. 2481.

growing presidential involvement in and leadership on such matters as postwar refugee policies.

To some extent, the executive-legislative conflict over immigration policy is but one facet of a larger ongoing struggle between the two branches for leadership in policymaking. However, other factors too have contributed significantly to the conflict—particularly the profoundly different perspectives of these two institutions with regard to immigration issues. The conflict between Congress and the executive on the subject of immigration has been at bottom one between domestic and international views of the issue.

Domestic Interests of Congress

Until recently Congress focused almost entirely on domestic considerations in making immigration policy, and its decisions represented efforts to accommodate the wide range of competing domestic interests rather than any clearly defined principles with respect to immigration. Thus, from its decision to exclude Chinese in 1882 to its abandonment of the national origins quota system in 1965, Congress mirrored the prevailing sentiment of the interested public. For example, congressional support of the anti-Chinese legislation came mainly from legislators from the far West, where the Chinese population was largest and the general hostility toward them most intense. According to political scientist Fred Riggs, members of Congress from other areas of the country supported Chinese exclusion but they were often indifferent to the issue.[19] Later, as prejudice against the new wave of supposedly inferior European immigrants developed and was supported by the country's social and intellectual elite,[20] legislators from the East joined the restrictionist effort. Opposition to the restrictionist pressures in Congress came mainly from representatives whose constit-

---

19. Fred Warren Riggs, *Pressures on Congress* (Greenwood Press, 1950), p. 23.
20. Barbara M. Solomon, "The Intellectual Background of the Immigration Restriction Movement in New England," *New England Quarterly*, vol. 25 (1952), pp. 47–59.

uencies included politically influential immigrant populations or businesses that relied on immigrant labor.

The domestic orientation of the Congress on this issue is further reflected in the several immigration studies it sponsored and in the character of its debates on major immigration laws between 1882 and 1952. Those studies invariably stressed the adverse effects of immigration on society and ignored the implications of highly restrictive policies for the country's image abroad or its foreign policy interests associated with immigration. To the extent that Congress did look abroad, it looked primarily for evidence to support its fears of inundation or subversion by immigrants.

This domestic focus began to change after World War II. Congress yielded to intense executive branch pressure for the repeal of the prohibition against Chinese immigration and for the extension of immigration quotas to India and the Philippines shortly after their independence. The damaging effects of the discriminatory national origins policy on U.S. foreign policy became a prominent issue in congressional deliberations on the McCarran-Walter Act. Congress rejected arguments against the quota system in 1952, but eventually acquiesced to the executive branch's position on the subject by discarding the system through the enactment of the Immigration and Nationality Act in 1965. Since then, congressional debates have paid increasing attention to the broad array of foreign policy interests on which immigration has some bearing and Congress sought to deal sensitively with some of them in its refugee legislation of 1980.

The predominantly domestic orientation of Congress in immigration matters is consistent with its tendency, noted by many analysts of congressional behavior, to focus on domestic or constituency concerns even in defense or foreign policy matters.[21] Such an orientation is understandable in the light of the local constituency pressures to which members of Congress

21. Lewis Anthony Dexter, "Congressmen and the Making of Military Policy," in Raymond Wolfinger, *Readings on Congress* (Prentice-Hall, 1971), p.372.

must respond. When there are strong, clear constituency preferences, an international orientation to immigration could be risky if the resulting policy was inconsistent with those local preferences. Of course, this clash between constituency interests and broader national or international interests is not peculiar to immigration matters. It is a common occurrence in national policymaking.

International Interests of the Executive

Presidents, on the other hand, usually have stressed international interests when they consider immigration issues. However, up to about 1945 presidents were by and large on the periphery of deliberations about immigration policy, their input confined to protesting congressional decisions thought to be injurious to the country's foreign policy interests, urging the adoption of specific measures, placating offended foreign governments, or vetoing unacceptable bills. At times these actions have had little effect on Congress. Yet, to the extent that a coherent set of beliefs, values, or objectives is identifiable in immigration policy, those have come mainly from the executive branch.

One of the country's first formal enunciations of a position on immigration came from the executive branch in the Burlingame Treaty of 1868 with China, in which the two countries agreed to acknowledge the right of individuals to emigrate and to permit unrestricted immigration by each other's nationals.[22] Some analysts suggest that this provision reflected Secretary of State William H. Seward's support for unrestricted immigration, particularly for the importation of cheap labor from China, and argue that it was not a carefully considered expression of an administration's position.[23] However, that position

22. "Treaty of Trade, Consuls and Emigration," *Treaties, Conventions, International Acts, Protocols and Agreements Between the United States and Other Powers, 1776–1909,* vol. 1 (GPO, 1910), p. 235.
23. Thomas Andrew Bailey, *A Diplomatic History of the American People* (Appleton-Century-Croft, 1955), pp. 336–37.

was clearly consistent with the democratic ideals of the country and has remained central to executive branch thinking about immigration policy since then even if it has not been reflected fully in official policies.

The Burlingame Treaty changed little on the U.S. side, since Chinese immigration had been increasing steadily before the treaty (during the 1860s it reached a peak of 64,300). When growing anti-Chinese sentiment in the 1870s led Congress to seek to ban further Chinese immigration, President Chester A. Arthur sought to avoid a major diplomatic embarrassment by discouraging such action. Failing to dissuade Congress, the president in 1882 negotiated with China a modification of the Burlingame Treaty that permitted the United States to suspend Chinese immigration without abrogating the treaty or creating a diplomatic crisis with China. In 1907 a similar problem developed when Congress moved to prohibit Japanese immigration. The president averted another diplomatic crisis by negotiating what came to be known as the "Gentlemen's Agreement" under which Japan agreed to voluntarily terminate Japanese migration to this country.

These were the first of several instances in which presidential and congressional attitudes toward immigration issues diverged sharply; the disagreements were to grow in depth and intensity. The numerous veto messages of presidents and the statements accompanying proposed immigration legislation consistently stressed that: (1) it is desirable to maintain the country's distinguished tradition of openness to immigrants; (2) the country's image abroad can be improved by eliminating discriminatory barriers to immigration; and (3) immigration can be an aid in pursuing broad U.S. foreign policy interests or in meeting specific obligations. Accordingly, presidents have opposed virtually all restrictive, discriminatory, or exclusionary immigration laws.

The executive branch fought hard to defeat legislation excluding Japanese as immigrants in 1935, warning of the severe adverse effects that such action would have on U.S.-Japanese relations. It lost that battle. Out of respect for the wartime alliance with China it fought equally hard—this time success-fully—to secure repeal of the Chinese exclusion law in 1943. And it persistently opposed the national origins principle used in establishing immigration quotas that proved to be increas-ingly embarrassing to the United States in its dealings with the countries adversely affected by the quota system. That embar-rassment grew as more and more countries outside of western Europe achieved independence and as U.S.-Soviet competition for influence among the newly emerging countries intensified after 1945. When in 1952 Congress ignored executive branch pleas to end the discriminatory policy and adopted the McCarran-Walter Act with those provisions, President Truman vetoed the bill. His veto message contains one of the clearest expres-sions of the executive's emphasis on the foreign policy aspects of immigration:

> What we do in the field of immigration and naturalization is vital to the continued growth and internal development of the United States—to the economic and social strength of our country—which is the core of the defense of the free world. Our immigration policy is equally, if not more important to the conduct of our foreign relations and to our responsibilities of moral leadership in the struggle for world peace.
>
> In one respect, this bill recognizes the great international significance of our immigration and naturalization policy, and takes a step to improve existing laws. All racial bars to natural-ization would be removed, and at least some minimum immi-gration quota would be afforded to each of the free nations of Asia. . . .
>
> But now this most desirable provision comes before me embedded in a mass of legislation which would perpetuate injustices of long standing against many other nations of the world, hamper the efforts we are making to rally the men of East and West alike to the cause of freedom, and intensify the repressive and inhumane aspects of our immigration proce-dures.[24]

24. "Veto of Bill to Revise the Laws Relating to Immigration, Naturalization, and Nationality, June 25, 1952," *Public Papers of the Presidents: Harry S. Truman, 1952–53* (GPO, 1966), pp. 441–47. (Hereafter *Public Papers: Truman, 1952–53*.)

A commission appointed by President Truman to study the country's immigration policy and recommend reforms further stressed the role of U.S. immigration policy in boosting the country's image abroad, noting in its January 1953 report that "the immigration law is an image in which other nations see us. It tells them how we really feel about them and their problems, and not how we say we do."[25]

For these reasons Presidents Eisenhower, Kennedy, and Johnson all urged that the discriminatory features of the immigration law be removed. In his January 13, 1965, message to Congress proposing immigration law reforms, President Johnson stated that the national origins quota system was "incompatible with our basic American tradition" and that "relationships with a number of countries, and hence the success of our foreign policy, is needlessly impeded" by it.[26] Testifying in 1964 before the House Committee on the Judiciary in support of the administration's proposals, Secretary of State Dean Rusk echoed this concern:

> We are concerned to see that our immigration laws reflect our real character and objectives because what other people think about us plays an important role in the achievement of our foreign policies. As long as our immigration law classifies persons according to national and ancestral origins, we cannot convince our critics that we judge each other on the basis of ability, industry, intelligence, integrity, and such other factors as determine a man's value to our society.[27]

Persuaded by these arguments, Congress in 1965 abandoned the national origins principle and other discriminatory features of immigration policy and enacted a law along the lines proposed by the president. As President Johnson stood in the shadow of the Statue of Liberty on New York's Ellis Island

25. *Whom We Shall Welcome, Report of the President's Commission on Immigration and Naturalization* (GPO, 1953), p. xiii.

26. "Special Message to the Congress on Immigration, January 13, 1965," *Public Papers of the Presidents: Lyndon B. Johnson, 1965* (GPO, 1966), vol. 1, p. 37.

27. *Immigration*, Hearings before Subcommittee No. 1 of the House Committee on the Judiciary, 89 Cong. 1 sess. (GPO, 1965), pt. 7, p. 88.

and signed into law the Immigration and Nationality Act of 1965, that moment marked the first time in the country's history that the two branches were in full agreement about the basic features of immigration policy.

This convergence of views was partly a result of the profound changes in public attitudes toward discrimination in public policy that occurred during the 1960s, when the civil rights movement challenged racial discrimination in public life and secured enactment of far-reaching civil rights and voting rights laws. An end to discrimination in immigration was but a logical step in this reform effort. It was also the result of increased congressional attention to U.S. relations with developing countries. Most important, the convergence of views was the result of a basic change in the dynamics of immigration that made old approaches inadequate, congressional dominance impractical, and presidential leadership unavoidable.

Largely because of the dislocations caused by the war, repression by newly installed communist regimes in some countries, and the severe economic hardships stemming from the war-ravaged European economies, most people who came to the United States immediately after the war were from precisely those countries against which immigration laws sought to discriminate. The admission of many of those uprooted and displaced people was an important aspect of the country's effort to stabilize western Europe and aid friendly countries in their recovery. As President Truman noted in his March 1952 message to Congress urging U.S. aid to European refugees:

> Overpopulation is one of the major factors preventing the fullest recovery of those countries where it exists. It is a serious drag on the economies of nations belonging to the North Atlantic Treaty Organization. A solution to this problem, therefore, becomes vitally necessary to strengthen the defense of the North Atlantic Community.[28]

This link between immigration and foreign policy, particu-

28. "Special Message to the Congress on Aid for Refugees and Displaced Persons, March 24, 1952," *Public Papers: Truman, 1952–53*, pp. 212–13.

larly national security policy, propelled the executive branch
into a leadership role in the formulation of immigration policy.
Between 1945 and 1948 more than 40,000 Europeans displaced
by the war were admitted to the country under an emergency
directive by the president. The 1948 Displaced Persons Act
passed at the request of President Truman allowed an additional
409,000 refugees to enter the country. Another 189,000 entered
under the Refugee Relief Act of 1953, passed at the urging of
President Dwight D. Eisenhower. Furthermore, an important
factor in the admission since the mid-1950s of more than 30,000
Hungarian refugees, 690,000 Cuban refugees, over 300,000
Indochinese refugees, and smaller numbers from virtually every
region of the world[29] has been the executive branch's initiative,
primarily through use of the parole authority of the attorney
general (established by the McCarran-Walter Act) in informal
consultation with Congress.

The Emerging Executive-Legislative Partnership

With the executive's growing influence on immigration
policy, something approaching a partnership has developed
between the executive branch and Congress. This partnership
was solidified by the Refugee Act of 1980.[30] Since the end of
World War II the executive branch had urged enactment of
refugee legislation that would increase the government's flexibility in responding to demands for refuge. The idea found
wide support in Congress but never enough to produce the
desired legislation. Thus the parole authority was the sole basis
for admitting large numbers of refugees. The 1980 Refugee
Act, the result of extensive executive-legislative collaboration,
provided for a much clearer and more orderly admission and
resettlement of refugees.

This law originated in bills introduced in the House by

29. *Review of U.S. Refugee Program and Policies,* Committee Print, prepared for the
Senate Committee on the Judiciary, 96 Cong. 2 sess. (GPO, 1970), p. 15.
30. Public Law 96-212 (codified in scattered sections of 8 U.S.C.).

Representative Joshua Eilberg, Democrat of Pennsylvania, and in the Senate by Senator Edward Kennedy, Democrat of Massachusetts. The administration outlined its proposals for a refugee law to the House Judiciary Committee's Subcommittee on Immigration, Citizenship, and International Law and to the appropriate congressional committee staff of both houses. The executive and Congress were in accord on virtually all major elements of a proposed refugee policy, and through informal discussions resolved differences on such specific points as the actual level of admissions to be allowed and the extent of resettlement assistance to be provided by the federal government. The refugee bill signed into law by President Jimmy Carter on March 17, 1980, not only reflected the best efforts of the executive branch and Congress, it established a framework for executive-legislative collaboration in making decisions about refugee admissions over and above the annual limit of 50,000 provided for by the law.

The differences between the executive branch and Congress over immigration have been narrowed considerably. While Congress now exhibits much greater sensitivity to international aspects of immigration policy, the president has also become more attentive to the domestic effects, especially with respect to refugee decisions. This convergence of views has improved the prospects for well-considered policies. However, it by no means ensures such policies. In virtually every area of immigration policy the issues are so complex and controversial that differences on specifics are inevitable. Furthermore, each branch retains a measure of suspicion about the political intentions of the other. These suspicions were demonstrated in the maneuverings over the Simpson-Mazzoli bill, which the House Speaker once blocked for fear the president planned to veto it in an attempt to win the support of Hispanic voters. Because any decision on the bill would have been controversial and perhaps costly in an election year, neither side wanted to expose itself to blame or to miss any benefits that might accrue from enactment.

The Changing Politics of Immigration Policy

How much immigration should occur, what types of people should come and under what circumstances, and what effects their coming is likely to have on the country have been and remain central issues in immigration policy. They have been difficult to answer because of the diverse interests that have been represented in the deliberations; the constantly changing social, economic, and demographic context in which these issues are debated; and society's continuing ambivalence about immigration and the complexity of the issues.

Not surprisingly, immigration policies have never reflected firm answers to these questions, but have been carefully contrived compromises among numerous interests and viewpoints. This outcome is not unique to immigration. On the contrary, it is the typical outcome in a pluralist polity. However, it ensures that the immigration dilemma will persist since such compromises invariably fail to be satisfactory remedies to the perceived problems. The protracted struggle to enact the Simpson-Mazzoli bill and the eventual failure to do so are only the most recent examples of the complex process of compromises that are required for even modest adjustments in policy.

But the absence of definitive remedies to problems should not obscure important and salutory changes in the process of decisionmaking. Three changes are especially noteworthy: (1) the mix of actors in the deliberations; (2) the salient issues in the debate; and (3) the character of the debate. While the mix of interest groups participating has not changed much, the influence of these groups has been changing. Nationalist-patriotic groups and their message of fear have yielded considerable ground to a wide assortment of humanitarian organizations seeking more generous and humane policies. Similarly, state and local governments have become increasingly active participants, largely as a result of their more active involvement with refugee resettlement and their concern about the costs to them of providing a wide range of public services to immigrants. Easily the most significant change in the influence of actors is the growing prominence of Mexican-Americans in the policy process. This development follows in the tradition of other ethnic groups who were active when they were a prominent part of the immigrant stream.

Another important change in the policy debate has to do with the specific concerns being addressed. Although some of the traditional policy concerns described earlier remain, three broad issues have been at the center of the current debate about immigration policy: controlling illegal immigration; the effect of immigrants on the economic opportunities of the domestic population and on the cost and availability of certain public services; and the civil rights of immigrants.

Since the early 1970s no issue in immigration policy has generated as much concern or received as much attention as has illegal immigration. This is so in part because more than any other immigration issue it reflects the inadequacies of current policies, the complex array of special interests in immigration matters, and the country's vulnerability to migration pressures outside its borders. The search for an effective and acceptable response to illegal immigration has been wide-ranging. The many possibilities that have been considered include measures that would improve the conditions in source countries that now push people to this country; strengthen U.S.-Mexico relations and their joint efforts to improve management of the southern border; and improve internal enforcement of immigration policies. The Simpson-Mazzoli immigration bill sought to adopt perhaps the mildest remedies likely to have an effect on the domestic front. While there has been wide consensus about the need for multilateral and bilateral efforts to deal with illegal immigration, no strategy has emerged for doing so.

A subject of increasing concern to the public and to policy-makers at every level of government is coping with the cost of providing immigrants with the basic social services—education, health care, and welfare benefits. One indication of this concern is the steps being taken in an increasing number of localities to monitor these costs and to explore the extent of local governments' responsibilities for providing these services. Another is the several bills introduced in Congress in recent years calling for the federal government to assume responsibility for medical and education costs imposed by immigrants and restricting access by immigrants to various cash assistance programs.[31] In addition, there have been repeated calls for better screening of immigrants to ensure that they do not become public charges and to enforce provisions for the expulsion of legal immigrants who do become public charges within five years of entry.[32]

This growing concern about the economic effects of immigration is based in part on the recent increases in immigration (especially in refugee admissions and illegal immigration) and on the rapidly rising cost of the social services that are now available to large segments of the population. As government officials at all levels seek to cope with these higher costs, attention tends to focus on users who might not be eligible. Although immigrants add only a minute share to the escalating costs in all but a few cases, they are a convenient target for complaints.[33]

Two broader issues are involved, however. First, to what extent should localities be required to assume the costs arising from the federal government's decision to admit immigrants

31. See H. Res. 2400, *Congressional Record*, vol. 123 (January 26, 1977), p. 2388; and H. Res. 3697, *Congressional Record*, vol. 123 (February 17, 1977), p. 4606. After two years of deliberation Congress amended the Social Security Act in 1980 to require that after September 30, 1980, immigrants who applied for public assistance should have their sponsor's income and resources imputed to them in the application for the first three years after entry.

32. H. Res. 8250, *Congressional Record*, vol. 123 (July 12, 1977), p. 22580.

33. For an indication of the extent of immigration participation in these programs, see Lenna Kennedy and Jack Schmulowitz, "SSI Payments to Lawfully Resident Aliens," *Social Security Bulletin*, vol. 43 (March 1980), pp. 3–10; and Henrietta J. Duvall, Karen W. Goudreau, and Robert E. Marsh, "Aid to Families with Dependent Children: Characteristics of Recipients in 1979," *Social Security Bulletin*, vol. 45 (April 1982), pp. 3–4.

or its failure to enforce its immigration laws effectively? Second, should the country, as host to immigrants, extend to them the full array of social benefits available to other residents and consider these costs offset by the benefits immigrants confer?

The civil rights of immigrants, particularly those who are in the country illegally, are also at the forefront of policy debate. Although some of the concerns here have been present for decades, especially in connection with the allegedly arbitrary practices of the INS in its investigative activities, they now cover a wider range of issues, including prolonged detention without hearing (as in the case of the Haitians and Mariel Bay Cubans who entered in 1980 without authorization but claim to be refugees) and the procedures by which claims are heard and decided on. Two other major issues in this area revolve around the procedures by which suspected illegal immigrants are apprehended and expelled and the risk that the rights of foreign-born Americans and legal immigrants will be violated through current enforcement practices or measures such as employer sanctions that aim to deny illegal immigrants access to the labor market. These civil rights issues—which are pursued most vigorously by Hispanics, blacks, and the American Civil Liberties Union—were some of the most sensitive and complex ones facing the Congress in its deliberations on the Simpson-Mazzoli bill. Furthermore, they have added to the complexity of the long-standing problem of how the government can accord certain basic rights to everyone under its jurisdiction and at the same time quickly and effectively enforce its immigration laws.

Perhaps the greatest change has come about in the tone and character of the debate. The bitter verbal assaults on the allegedly inferior races and cultures gaining entry and the shrill expressions of fear for the well-being of the society have all but disappeared from public discussion. The deliberations of the past decade about refugee admissions, illegal immigration, and broader immigration reform have been characterized, on the whole, by a civility and sensitivity that eloquently testify to profound changes in the country's attitudes toward race and culture. Although prejudice and bitterness crop up from time to time in specific localities as groups compete for or respond to perceived inequities in the distribution of scarce benefits, the changed tone of the national debate suggests that politicians are not likely to make any gains by injecting these attitudes into national immigration policy debates.

The changed character of the public debate also reflects the greater scope of immigration policy today. Few federal government officials are unaware of or unconcerned about the sweeping international implications of U.S. immigration policy decisions or of the level of attention policy deliberations receive abroad. Even though the Simpson-Mazzoli bill maintained an almost exclusively domestic focus, virtually all those who considered it acknowledged the broader global issues that remain to be addressed and perceived the bill as one of several major efforts necessary to deal responsibly with current immigration issues.

3

The Pattern of Immigration: How Much, Who, and Why

THE central questions in the formulation of U.S. immigration policy—how much should occur and what kind of people should come—have never been easy to answer. Policymakers have had to change their minds many times over the years in their search for satisfactory answers. Not only have they had to respond to changing social attitudes, economic conditions, and domestic and international political considerations, but to some extent the dynamics of the immigration process itself have determined the answers. Because these developments directly affect the administration of immigration policy, the problems of administration cannot be analyzed without attention to them, to current immigration trends, and to the outlook for future trends in the level and composition of immigration.

How Much Immigration

Although Congress has imposed numerical limits on immigration since 1921, those limits have never been firm. As a result of various exemptions from the ceiling, legislation by Congress authorizing admission of special groups outside the ceiling, and administrative actions modifying the ceiling, actual immigration has routinely exceeded the ceiling. Between 1971 and 1980, for example, the annual ceiling stipulated by law totaled 290,000, whereas actual legal immigration averaged about 450,000 per year and reached 601,000 in 1978.[1] If all refugees and illegal aliens were included, total immigration would probably be about 1 million a year—which is more than three times the current ceiling.[2]

The discrepancy between the legislated ceiling and actual immigration results in part from a deliberate choice by policymakers to exempt some countries or categories of immigrants from the ceiling and to retain some flexibility to respond to special situations. It is also a result of this country's increasing inability to enforce its policies effectively in the face of strong emigration pressures abroad and its continuing need for more and different types of immigrants than the law provides. Thus, largely to avoid offending the self-governing Western Hemisphere countries, these countries were exempted from numerical ceilings until the 1965 immigration law established a 120,000 ceiling for the Western Hemisphere with no country limitation or preference system involved. Some categories of immigrants, such as spouses and children of U.S. citizens and parents of adult citizens, have always been exempt from the ceiling. In addition, Congress has authorized admission of several groups of refugees since 1946 over and above the existing ceiling, totaling more than 1.5 million between 1946 and 1980. The 1980 Refugee Act provided considerable flexibility by authorizing the president to exceed a ceiling of 50,000 refugees after appropriate consultations with Congress. In these several actions, Congress has displayed a strong preference for flexi-

1. Immigration statistics not cited by footnotes are from the Immigration and Naturalization Service, *1981 Statistical Yearbook.*

2. Under current law, immigrants are aliens admitted lawfully for permanent residence. Refugees are permitted to change their status to that of immigrants after one year in the country. Illegal immigrants have no legal status and usually are expelled upon detection. Both refugees and illegal immigrants are classified as immigrants here because their behavior and effects on society are in most respects those of immigrants.

bility in the number of immigrants admitted. It demonstrated that preference again when the House quickly deleted from the Senate-approved version of the Simpson-Mazzoli bill a proposed firm ceiling of 425,000 immigrants a year.

By far the greatest concern with respect to the level of immigration has been the high incidence of illegal entrants, both those who later seek refugee status and those who remain surreptitiously. While the former occurrence on a large scale is a relatively new phenomenon, the latter has been occurring in varying degrees ever since the country sought to restrict access. No one knows how many immigrants are in the country illegally or at what rate their numbers are growing. Several estimates have been made on the basis of census data or the number of illegal immigrants apprehended by the Immigration and Naturalization Service (INS) annually, but the estimates vary widely.

The total number of illegal immigrants apprehended by the INS soared to 8.3 million in 1971–80, up from 1.6 million in the previous decade. Moreover, in 1981, 975,780 illegal immigrants were apprehended, down from a peak of 1.07 million in 1979, but more than twice the number for 1971. Most of the allegations of large-scale illegal immigration have been based on these figures. Although these statistics strongly suggest a high level of illegal immigration, considerably more information is needed to produce reliable estimates of its actual level.

Some census-based estimates of illegal immigration are probably slightly more informative, but their numerous limitations make them only marginally useful. For one thing, illegal immigrants are unlikely to report their illegal status to an enumerator. For another, the Census Bureau has no way of estimating how many illegal immigrants were enumerated and what proportion of the whole the enumerated population represents. A number of recent evaluations of the disparate and fragmentary evidence available have suggested that the illegal immigrant population ranges from 2.5 million to 6 million.[3] One recent estimate of the number counted by the 1980 census was 2.047 million.[4] It is derived from actual census data and annual alien registrations and is considered the most reliable low-end estimate available. Although it is not known what proportion of the total population it represents, this estimate does provide some reasonably sound information about this segment of the immigrant population. It indicates that the illegal population exceeds 2 million and, because it is likely that a large number (probably half of that population) would avoid enumeration, a population of 4 million in 1980 seems a justifiable assumption.

Of course, this estimate represents the population in place at the time of the census. No one knows the annual net flow and thus the rate at which the illegal immigrant population is growing. The estimated census enumeration provides at least some indication of the pace of growth between 1960 and 1980. It calculates that 570,000 illegal immigrants entered during 1960–69 and that 1.4 million entered during 1970–80 (of which 890,000 entered between 1975 and 1980).[5] If a 50 percent enumeration is again assumed, the illegal population appears to have risen by about 355,000 annually during the second half of the 1970s. When the continuing high level of apprehensions is also taken into account (more than 1 million were apprehended in 1979), it appears that the illegal immigrant population has risen from about 4 million in 1980 to above 5 million in 1983.

These various estimates have helped to strengthen the belief that too much immigration is occurring and that the country is increasingly unable to control it. But exactly what amount is

3. For a review of the major attempts to estimate the size of the illegal alien population, see General Accounting Office, *Problems and Options in Estimating the Size of the Illegal Alien Population*, IPE-82-9 (GAO, 1982), pp. 26–27.

4. Robert Warren and Jeffrey S. Passel, "Estimates of Illegal Aliens from Mexico Counted in the 1980 United States Census," paper prepared for the 1983 annual meeting of the Population Association of America.

5. Ibid.

too much? That question is almost impossible to answer because there are no criteria for determining appropriate levels.

Annual ceilings established in the past have not been based on any assessment of the country's absorptive capacity or explicit growth targets. The drive to restrict immigration in 1921, for example, was prompted by the general fear that large-scale immigration was harmful for the country. But neither the ceilings established in 1921 and 1924 nor the formula used to arrive at them reflected any calculations of the country's desired growth rate, domestic needs, or absorptive capacity. When in 1951 the Truman Commission on Immigration was told by several witnesses that the country could absorb several hundred thousand immigrants annually without adverse effects, it nonetheless recommended an annual ceiling of only 251,000 (one-sixth of 1 percent of the 1950 population), which it considered to be "fully within the capacity of the United States in the foreseeable future."[6] The immigration law passed by Congress in 1952 ignored all of this, however, and imposed a ceiling of 154,000. This arbitrary approach was taken again in the 1960s. In its report on the 1964 immigration and nationality bill, the House Judiciary Committee stated that its proposed annual ceiling of 170,000 for immigrants from Eastern Hemisphere countries represented the country's maximum absorptive capacity, but it offered no basis for this determination and indeed seemed to have had none.[7] Congress subsequently adopted a ceiling of 170,000 for the Eastern Hemisphere in 1965 and fixed a ceiling of 120,000 for the Western Hemisphere, but postponed a decision about whether the Western Hemisphere ceiling would be imposed until 1968, when, in spite of strong State Department opposition, Congress authorized it. When in 1978 the Select Commission on Immigration and Refugee Policy was

6. *Whom We Shall Welcome: Report of the President's Commission on Immigration and Naturalization* (Government Printing Office, 1953), p. 81.

7. *Amending the Immigration and Nationality Act, and for Other Purposes,* H. Rept. 745, 89 Cong. 1 sess. (GPO, 1965), p. 13.

also asked to consider how much immigration is prudent, it recommended a ceiling of 425,000 inclusive of some refugee admissions, not on the basis of a reasoned appraisal of the country's capacity to absorb immigrants but on an arbitrary judgment about what the country would find acceptable in 1980.[8]

How much immigration the country can prudently permit remains a hotly debated issue. Although public officials still cannot even agree on the criteria that should guide such a determination, two factors have been emphasized often: the degree to which the labor market can absorb immigrant workers without imposing undue hardships on existing workers; and the effect of immigration on the country's population growth. However, controversy surrounds these points as well. Some analysts believe that immigrants expand the labor market and therefore help rather than hurt domestic workers, whereas others believe that, overall, immigrants tend to displace domestic workers. As chapter 2 indicates, the effects of immigration on the labor market are still unclear.

Opinions are also divided on the desirability of population growth. Some analysts consider any significant growth to be harmful, whereas others consider modest growth beneficial. If total net annual immigration is assumed to be 750,000 (a Census Bureau estimate that predicts continued high inflows of refugees and illegal aliens), then the population of the United States in the year 2000 would be over 274 million. This figure would amount to an increase of about 16 million people or a 6 percent rise above the projected population if there were no net immigration growth after 1982.[9] Whether or not this is too

8. Larry H. Fuchs, "The Current Policy Debate on Illegal Immigration," paper prepared for the Wingspread Workshop on Labor Market Impacts of Immigration, August 3, 1982.

9. The estimated 750,000 total net immigration is composed of 880,000 legal immigrants, refugees, Cubans, and illegal aliens; 25,000 civilian citizens; 5,000 Puerto Ricans; and 160,000 outmigrants. Bureau of the Census, *Current Population Reports*, series P-25, "Projections of the Population of the United States, by Age, Sex, and Race: 1983 to 2080" (GPO, 1984), pp. 13, 19.

much immigration depends on what is considered a desirable rate of population growth. The country has never come close to formulating such a standard. Thus the answer to how much immigration should be allowed is likely to continue to be determined by the interplay of the many forces that have traditionally influenced immigration policy.

Who Should Come

The United States became selective about its immigrants well before it managed to impose numerical limits. Starting in about 1882, several immigration laws established qualitative restrictions. By 1920 immigrants were required to be literate, have good health and character, be free of association with communist or other radical political organizations, and to be of certain racial or ethnic origin. The objectives, broadly, were to reduce the cost of immigration to the society and particularly to host cities, protect the national security, and reduce the level of immigration. Many of these restrictions remain in force and the broad objectives are the same, but some important changes have occurred as well.

Among the most noteworthy changes are the removal of restrictions against some racial or ethnic populations, increased emphasis on admitting relatives of citizens and resident aliens (family reunification), and a sharp reduction in the proportion of immigrants admitted specifically as workers. These changes—instituted primarily by means of the "preference system," which allocates the total number of authorized immigrant visas among specified categories of aliens—have substantially altered the composition of the immigrant stream. In 1952, when labor force augmentation was still regarded as a major objective of U.S. immigration policy, 50 percent of all visas were reserved for highly skilled or educated immigrants (workers). After the 1965 law increased the emphasis on family reunification, 74 percent of all visas were reserved for relatives of U.S. residents,

Table 3-1. *Preference Categories for U.S. Immigration, 1984*

Preference category[a]	Percent of total ceiling of 270,000[b]
First preference: unmarried sons and daughters (over 21 years of age) of U.S. citizens	20
Second preference: spouses and unmarried sons and daughters of aliens lawfully admitted for permanent residence	26
Third preference: members of the professions or persons of exceptional ability in the sciences and arts	10
Fourth preference: married sons and daughters of U.S. citizens	10
Fifth preference: brothers and sisters of U.S. citizens 21 years of age or over	24
Sixth preference: skilled and unskilled workers in short supply	10

Source: 8 U.S.C. 1153(a).
a. Unused visas in all but the two occupational categories (third and sixth preference) are passed to the next preference category.
b. Refugee Act of 1980, Public Law 96-212 (codified in scattered sections of 8 U.S.C.). In addition to broadening the definition of refugee status, this statute eliminated a seventh preference category, increased the second preference from 20 to 26 percent, and reduced the worldwide ceiling for the remaining six from 290,000 to 270,000.

20 percent for skilled and unskilled individuals in fields in which a labor shortage existed in the United States and members of the learned professions who have exceptional ability, and 6 percent for refugees. The Refugee Act of 1980 gave refugees a special status outside the preference system and thus reallocated the remaining preferences to relatives of U.S. residents (table 3-1).

These changes have helped to reduce the controversy about who comes and given clearer purpose to immigration, but the new distribution of preferences is probably less significant than the numbers suggest. Most immigrants who came before 1965 as workers were probably joining relatives, while most of those who now come on the basis of family ties enter the labor market soon after entry.[10] Similarly, even though the country only recently began to reserve a substantial proportion of each year's visas for refugees, the history of immigration has been one of refuge to many threatened or persecuted individuals.

10. National Commission for Manpower Policy, *Manpower and Population Policies in the United States*, no. 20 (GPO, 1978), pp. 92–98.

Sources of Immigration

The sharp rise in total immigration in recent years has been accompanied by a considerable change in the ethnic composition of the immigrant population being admitted. Between 1931 and 1960 the majority of the immigrants admitted were from Europe: 41 percent of all immigrants came from northern and western Europe, 17 percent came from southern and eastern Europe, and only 5 percent from Asia (figure 3-1). By 1977–79 only 13 percent of the immigrants were from all of Europe, whereas 81 percent came from the developing countries of Asia and Latin America (including Mexico and the Caribbean basin).

This shift is not surprising if it is viewed in its historical perspective. There have been three main waves of immigration in the history of the United States, each originating from a different primary area. The first wave, which began in the 1840s and lasted until about 1890, came from northern and western Europe (principally Germany, the United Kingdom, Ireland, and the Scandinavian countries); the second wave, which spanned the period from 1890 to about 1965, came from southern and eastern Europe; and the third and current wave is coming from Asia, Latin America, and the Caribbean. The current flow is partly a product of the Immigration and Nationality Act of 1965 (as amended), which discarded the national origins principle and allowed a maximum of 20,000 qualified immigrants from each Eastern Hemisphere country, with no per country limit for the Western Hemisphere. As in the past, however, the pattern of global political and economic development has played an important role here.

Immigration from the Asian countries—notably India and Vietnam—has increased more than twentyfold since 1965, the sharpest increase during this period. Between 1977 and 1979 alone the share of total immigration from Asian countries was 39 percent, or three times that in the 1960s. The flow from

Figure 3-1. *Immigrants Admitted to the United States, by Region of Birth, 1820–1979*

Percent

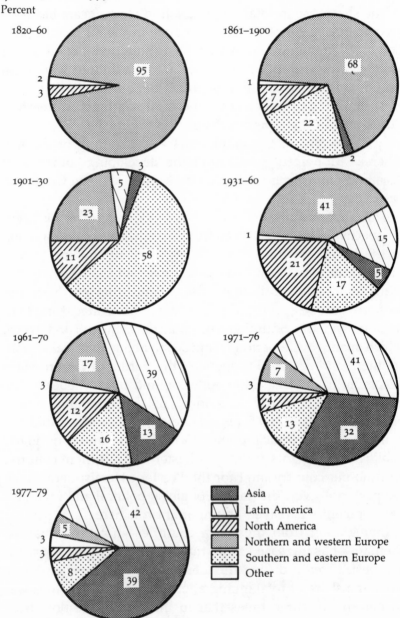

Source: Leon F. Bouvier and Cary B. Davis, *The Future Racial Composition of the United States* (Washington, D.C.: Population Reference Bureau, 1982), p. 2.

Latin America, including Mexico, the West Indies, and South America, rose by 112 percent between 1965 and 1978, and for some Caribbean countries like Trinidad and Tobago and Jamaica the increases exceeded 900 percent (table 3-2). Of course, the percentage increases are very high in some cases because the pre-1965 base was extremely low.

The same shifts in the source countries supplying legal immigrants have occurred in those supplying refugees and illegal immigrants. In fact, the recent flow pattern is largely the result of a change in refugee sources. Before 1960 the majority of refugees came from eastern Europe and the Soviet Union. Almost all of the approximately 523,000 refugees admitted to the United States under the Displaced Persons Act of 1948, the Refugee Relief Act of 1953, and the Refugee-Escapee Act of 1960 were Europeans. Starting with the great influx of Cubans during the 1960s, however, more and more refugees have been from developing countries. The overwhelming majority of the approximately 881,000 refugees admitted between 1960 and 1981 came from these countries. Of course, three Southeast Asian countries—Vietnam, Cambodia, and Laos—were by far the most prominent sources, but the stream of refugees from the Caribbean basin has been steadily growing as well.

Although the origins of illegal immigrants cannot be established with certainty, two sets of data—from the INS and the Census Bureau—strongly suggest that the majority come from developing countries. When countries are ranked by the average annual expulsions of their nationals as reported by the INS, nine of the top ten during the past ten years have been neighboring Western Hemisphere countries. The 1980 census confirms this pattern in that more than half of the 2.047 million illegal immigrants enumerated are from North and Central American countries (including the Caribbean); 40 percent or more are from Mexico alone. Asia, Europe, South America, and Oceania trail far behind.[11]

11. Warren and Passel, "Estimates of Illegal Aliens," table 3.

Table 3-2. *Immigrants Admitted to the United States, by Country or Region of Birth, Fiscal Years 1965 and 1978*

Country of birth	Number		Percent change
	1965	1978	
Europe	113,424	73,198	−35.5
Austria	1,680	467	−72.2
Belgium	1,005	439	−56.3
Czechoslovakia	1,894	744	−60.7
Denmark	1,384	409	−70.4
France	4,039	1,844	−54.3
Germany	24,045	6,739	−72.0
Greece	3,002	7,035	134.3
Hungary	1,574	941	−40.2
Ireland	5,463	1,180	−78.4
Italy	10,821	7,415	−31.5
Netherlands	3,085	1,153	−62.6
Norway	2,256	423	−81.3
Poland	8,465	5,050	−40.3
Portugal	2,005	10,445	420.9
Romania	1,644	2,037	23.9
Spain	2,200	2,297	4.4
Sweden	2,411	638	−73.5
Switzerland	1,984	706	−64.4
U.S.S.R.	1,853	5,161	178.5
United Kingdom	27,358	14,245	−47.9
Yugoslavia	2,818	2,621	−7.0
Other Europe	2,438	1,209	−50.4
Asia	20,683	249,776	1,107.6
China and Taiwan	4,057	21,315	425.4
Hong Kong	712	5,158	624.4
India	582	20,753	3,465.8
Iran	804	5,861	629.0

Characteristics of Immigrants

The drastic shift in the sources of immigration since 1965 has meant an equally drastic change in the languages and cultures being absorbed by this country. For one thing, an extremely large proportion—more than 40 percent of the approximately 8 million legal and illegal immigrants counted by the census in 1980—are now Spanish-speaking.[12] Although major cultural differences exist within this Spanish-speaking

12. Ibid., tables 2 and 3.

Table 3-2 (*continued*)

Country of birth	Number 1965	Number 1978	Percent change
Japan	3,180	4,010	26.1
Korea	2,165	29,288	1,252.8
Pakistan	187	3,876	1,972.7
Philippines	3,130	37,216	1,089.0
Thailand	214	3,574	1,570.1
Vietnam	226	88,543	39,078.3
Other Asia	5,426	30,182	456.2
North America	126,729	220,778	74.2
Canada	38,327	16,863	−56.0
Mexico	37,969	92,367	143.3
West Indies	37,583	91,361	143.1
Cuba	19,760	29,754	50.6
Dominican Republic	9,504	19,458	104.7
Haiti	3,609	6,470	79.3
Jamaica	1,837	19,265	948.7
Trinidad and Tobago	485	5,973	1,131.5
Other West Indies	2,388	10,441	337.2
Other North America	12,850	20,187	57.1
South America	30,962	41,764	34.9
Argentina	6,124	3,732	−39.1
Brazil	2,869	1,923	−33.0
Colombia	10,885	11,032	1.4
Other South America	11,084	25,077	126.2
Africa	3,383	11,524	240.6
Oceania	1,512	4,402	191.1
Other countries	4	. . .	. . .
All countries	296,697	601,442	102.7

Source: Immigration and Naturalization Service, *1978 Statistical Yearbook*, table 1A.

segment of the immigrant population, it is a highly visible population bloc and as such helps to reinforce the public perception that immigration has been increasing rapidly and creating a large new language minority.

Up to World War II, newly arrived immigrants were more likely to be low-skilled males of primary labor force age (between fourteen and forty-four) than was the U.S. population as a whole. For legal immigrants, this trend no longer holds. By 1950 the average immigrant was almost twice as likely to be a professional or technical worker as was the average U.S.

Table 3-3. *Immigrants Admitted to the United States, by Age,*
1899–1948 and 1966–78
Percent

Age group	1899–1948	1966–78
Under 16 years	13.9	26.5
16–44 years	79.0	58.8
45 years and older	7.1	14.6

Sources: For 1899–1948, *The Immigration and Naturalization Systems of the United States*, S. Rept. 1515, 81 Cong. 2 sess. (GPO, 1950), p. 157. For 1966–78, Immigration and Naturalization Service, *1978 Statistical Yearbook*, table 10; and INS, *1975 Annual Report*, table 10.

resident. In recent years the immigrant population, although it has remained well above the national average, has come to resemble the general population more. Similarly, the proportion of immigrants between the ages of sixteen and forty-four was considerably higher than the national average during the first five decades of this century, but since 1965 the proportion of youths under sixteen and of adults over forty-five has almost doubled, probably as a result of the increased emphasis on family reunification (table 3-3). Although at present it is impossible to determine whether or to what extent illegal immigrants differ from the legal immigrant population in this respect, the available evidence suggests that illegal immigrants are likely to be less well educated and to be mainly of labor force age.

Why Immigrants Come

That overall immigration levels have far exceeded the annual ceilings established by law since World War II is an indication not only of the flexibility of the legislated ceilings, but also of the powerful forces in this country and abroad that have led immigrants to seek entry to the United States. What these forces are, how they operate, and the extent to which they are susceptible to control by official actions are questions that need to be considered in any discussion of this country's immigration experience and the prospects for achieving more effective control in the future.

The basic forces behind international migration are widely known, but much remains unknown about the specific conditions or perceptions that cause individuals to migrate or about the relative weight of these factors in their decisions. Most analysts of international migration use a "push-pull" model to explain the phenomenon. The model is based on the hypothesis that people migrate when unsatisfactory political, social, or economic conditions push or encourage them to leave their homeland and when promising economic opportunities or a more hospitable political and social climate in another country pull or attract them there.[13] Some analysts consider this push-pull phenomenon to be a feature of the dependency relationships between highly developed capitalist countries and developing countries.[14]

Although the push-pull model sheds some light on international migration, it does not fully explain the phenomenon. The push-pull forces must affect millions of people throughout the world, yet only a small number migrate. Those who do migrate often have the benefit of special circumstances or facilitating conditions that make migration feasible. Thus the forces that contribute to immigration must include the facilitating conditions as well as the push-and-pull forces.

The Development Syndrome as Push

The current influx of immigrants from developing countries is neither a surprising nor a new phenomenon. Now, as in the past, the principal patterns of immigration coincide with the broad path of economic development throughout the world. Immigration from northern and western Europe before 1880 was the result of economic, political, and social factors linked with the rapid industrialization and urbanization that accom-

---

13. Alejandro Portes, "International Labor Migration and National Development," in Mary Kritz, ed., *U.S. Immigration and Refugee Policy: Global and Domestic Issues* (Lexington Books, 1983), pp. 71–76.
14. Ibid., pp. 76–81.

panied the industrial revolution. In some countries emigration was pushed by specific economic crises, such as the potato famine that wracked Ireland in the 1840s. In most countries, however, it was stimulated by the demographic, economic, and social forces unleashed by economic development.

As northern and western European societies overcame the turbulence of the demographic and economic transformation brought about by rapid industrialization and as their modern economies became stabilized, the immigration stream from these areas leveled off and then receded. As economic development gradually moved southward and eastward in Europe in an expanding economic revolution, southern and eastern Europe became the principal sources of an unprecedented flow of immigrants. They continued to come in large numbers between 1890 and 1920 even though an increasingly concerned America sought to discourage the flow. One scholar described the relationship between economic development in Europe and migration as follows:

> Paradoxically, it was the initial incursions of modern technology that gave rise to the emigration impetus. As the influence of modernism spread eastward and southward, the most readily assimilable life-sustaining features of the process gave rise to the dramatic mortality changes. . . . The rapid population growth that ensued created a deteriorating economic situation that could not, during the early periods, be ameliorated within the confines of the existing institutions of hitherto relatively unmodernized societies. Emigration thus followed the spread of modern economic development from its centers in northern and western Europe to the peripheries of the continent.[15]

After a temporary slump during World War I, immigration from southern and eastern Europe continued at a high rate up to 1928. It declined sharply between 1928 and 1945 as a result of the numerical restrictions imposed by the United States in 1924, the severe depression that began there in 1929, and discouragement of emigration by Italy's new Fascist government. After World War II immigration picked up again and

---

15. Gerald Rosenblum, *Immigrant Workers: Their Impact on American Labor Radicalism* (Basic Books, 1973), p. 48.

continued at a high rate throughout most of the 1950s. This time the flow was primarily the result of the dislocations and economic hardships brought on by the war.

By the 1960s the economies of the European countries had almost recovered from the effects of the war and some countries (such as Germany, Switzerland, and the Scandinavian countries) were enjoying rapid industrial growth, which allowed them to absorb many of the migrants from the poorer European countries; thus immigration from Europe to the United States declined. When, however, the United States abandoned the national origins principle and raised the annual ceiling on immigration in the Immigration and Nationality Act of 1965, immigration from the developing countries of Asia and the Caribbean basin increased sharply. In these new major source countries, as had been the case earlier in the European countries, the beginning of rapid economic development created conditions that induced massive emigration. In some, notably the Commonwealth Caribbean countries, large-scale migration to the United Kingdom and Canada already had been under way and much of that flow merely shifted to the United States when it became accessible and when the United Kingdom sharply curtailed immigration.

The relationship between economic development and migration is not entirely clear. However, a substantial body of research has suggested that rapid economic development is highly disruptive and forces people to abandon traditional values and life-styles for new ones, replacing much of the labor-intensive modes of production with capital-intensive production and thereby displacing many workers. Accordingly, those who are able to find employment will have increased earnings and thus will be able to afford to emigrate. Economic development also brings with it improved communications, transportation facilities, rapid population growth, rapid urbanization, and heightened public aspirations.[16]

16. See, for example, Marion J. Levy, Jr., *Modernization and the Structure of Society* (Princeton University Press, 1966), vol. 1, pp. 237–39; and Everett Lee, "A Theory of Migration," *Demography*, vol. 3 (1966), pp. 47–57.

Much of the current international migration, particularly migration to the United States, is the result of continued economic development around the world. Deep, widespread concern over continued poverty and over the inability of many countries to meet basic human needs tends to obscure the fact that since the end of World War II most of the non-European countries have experienced substantial and sustained economic development. Even Haiti, one of the poorest and most economically stagnant countries in the world, experienced a respectable 2.1 percent average annual rate of growth in GNP between 1970 and 1976.[17] According to one source, developing countries experienced an average annual growth rate of 5.7 percent a year between 1970 and 1976, an overall performance unmatched by what are now the developed countries.[18] Thus most of the principal sources of immigration at present are countries that have experienced substantial economic development over the past twenty-five years.

Unemployment and Low Wages

Developing countries invariably have very high rates of unemployment and underemployment, a problem that has grown worse since the mid-1970s and thus has given rise to increased migration pressures. Because consistent and comparable data on the labor force and employment are extremely difficult to obtain for these countries, the full extent of the problem is all but impossible to assess. However, it is evident that most of these countries have moderate to extremely high rates of unemployment and pervasive underemployment.[19] Several countries that report moderate levels of unemployment also report very high rates of underemployment. A Chilean program operating under the auspices of the International

17. World Bank, *1983 World Bank Atlas*, p. 20.
18. World Bank, *World Development Report, 1979*, p. 3.
19. David Morawetz, *Twenty-five Years of Economic Development, 1950 to 1975* (World Bank, 1977).

Labor Organization found that a group of seventeen Latin American countries averaged an estimated 6 percent unemployment and 27 percent underemployment in the early 1970s. The pattern was the same for Mexico.[20] The relatively low unemployment and high underemployment rates for most of these countries reflect the fact that a large proportion of the work force classified as underemployed is engaged in occasional, low-wage, subsistence labor—eking out an existence on the streets or through brief stints at seasonal agricultural work—because of the absence of virtually any form of public assistance to the unemployed.

Closely related to the unemployment-underemployment problem in these developing countries is that of low wages. Standard measures of per capita income fail to reflect the size of the disparities between the earnings of workers in the developing and developed countries because in most of these developing countries a small proportion of the working population earns the bulk of total incomes while a very large proportion earns the remaining small share.

Extremely high unemployment and underemployment combined with low wages constitute a barrier to the fulfillment of the aspirations of millions of people. To an even greater extent than the unemployed, the underemployed or inadequately paid worker is likely to seek better economic opportunities by migrating. Because these conditions serve as major push forces, the pressures for entry to this country are not likely to subside soon; the employment and wage levels in these countries will probably not improve significantly in the near future. If anything, many of these countries have been losing ground to the developed countries in recent years in employment and pay for their working-age populations. This widening opportunity gap makes the labor markets of developed countries such as the United States increasingly attractive. Migration is therefore becoming an increasingly rational economic investment for the

20. J. J. Buttari, ed., *El Problema Ocupacional en América Latina*, vol. 1: *Mano de Obra y Empleo* (Argentina: Ediciones S.I.A.P., 1978), p. 422.

nationals of developing countries, even at the risk and presumably high cost of illegal entry.

Population Growth

One of the great benefits of development since 1945 has been a lowering of mortality rates as modern science and increased health education globally have combined to eradicate or control many once-devastating diseases. That factor and the relatively high birthrates of many developing countries have kept their populations growing at a fairly brisk rate. According to a recent survey, the rate of population growth in all developing countries fell only slightly between 1960 and 1980, from 2.4 to 2.2 percent.[21] In Latin America and the Caribbean the rate dipped from 2.8 percent in 1961–65 to 2.3 in 1977 and since then has remained largely unchanged.[22] The high growth rates and relative youthfulness of the population of these countries mean that governments will find it increasingly difficult to create employment opportunities and provide for the basic needs of their people.

In the past the surplus labor of countries with high population growth rates could be absorbed by developed countries with far lower population growth rates and severe labor shortages. Now, however, most developed countries are unwilling or unable to absorb large numbers of immigrant workers because of declining rates of economic growth and growing concern about the social and ecological consequences of such immigration.[23] This is the case particularly in the countries of western Europe, which have sharply curtailed some immigration and the admission of guest workers. Reduced migration opportu-

21. United Nations, International Economic and Social Affairs Department, *World Population Trends and Policies: 1981 Monitoring Report*, vol. 2 (New York: United Nations, 1982), p. 4.

22. United Nations, International Economic and Social Affairs Department, *International Migration Policies and Programmes: A World Survey* (New York: United Nations, 1982), pp. 20–39.

23. Chandra Hardy, "Mexico's Development Strategy for the 1980s," *World Development*, vol. 10 (June 1982), p. 503.

nities in turn intensify the pressures created by large populations in the developing countries and thus help to impede their social and economic advancement. As U.S. Ambassador Richard E. Benedick recently pointed out to the U.N. Population Commission, not only are current high levels of population growth aggravating already unacceptably high levels of unemployment and underemployment, but the rise of crowded megacities "will bring hitherto unimagined problems and increase the potential for social unrest. . . . Never in human history has there been such a discrepancy between the supply of and the demand for international migration."[24]

Mexico is a prime example of a country in which rapid population growth alongside limited economic opportunities has created intense migration pressures. Mexico's annual average growth rate was 0.9 percent between 1910 and 1940, but it shot up to 2.7 percent during 1941–50 and reached an alarming 3.4 percent in 1970; at that rate the country's population would have doubled in about twenty-one years. In 1972 the Mexican government abandoned its pronatalist policies and launched a major family planning effort that yielded impressive results by the end of the 1970s. Although the average for the decade was still up around 3.3 percent, by 1979 the growth rate reportedly had fallen to 2.7 percent.[25]

Despite substantial reductions in the population growth rate over the past few years, Mexico's population of 75.7 million in mid-1983 is expected to reach 115 million by the year 2000.[26] The anticipated income from oil and natural gas will probably do little for the unemployment situation here since Mexico's labor force—according to one estimate in 1980—is growing at the rate of about 900,000 a year, whereas participation in the

24. U.S. Department of State, *Population Growth and Foreign Policy*, Current Policy Series, 263 (January 27, 1981).

25. Thomas G. Exter, "Demographics of Mexico," *American Demographics*, vol. 4 (February 1982), p. 23; and Population Reference Bureau, *1983 World Population Data Sheet* (Washington, D.C.: PRB, 1983).

26. Population Reference Bureau, *1983 World Population Data Sheet*.

labor force is only around 29 percent.[27] Even if the population growth rate declined further in the 1980s, Mexico would have to create more than 800,000 jobs annually to accommodate the expected increase in the labor force, but less than half that number will probably be available, according to the most optimistic projections. Thus there is every reason to believe that the number of Mexican workers wanting to enter the United States to find employment will continue to increase rapidly.

Although the other Central American countries do not have nearly as large a population as that of Mexico, they too are experiencing relatively brisk growth, which in 1983 alone was calculated to be 2.7 percent.[28] This level is unlikely to fall significantly in the near future. Because many of these countries are already densely populated and possess limited resources, they will be hard pressed indeed to provide for the basic needs of their population. Migration opportunities are therefore likely to be increasingly important to them.

Political Conditions

International migration is also strongly influenced by political conditions, which are thought to have been among the most powerful push forces in the past:

> The most dramatic twentieth-century change in European migration patterns was . . . the expanding role of political pressures and political controls. Politics impinged upon migration in three distinct ways: through war, through deliberate relocation of ethnic minorities, and through stringent national controls over immigration and emigration.[29]

Political turmoil has been particularly prominent in the developing countries whose political systems are still fragile and

27. Hardy, "Mexico's Development Strategy," p. 503.
28. Population Reference Bureau, *1983 World Population Data Sheet.*
29. Charles Tilley, "Migration in Modern European History," in William McNeil and Ruth S. Adams, eds., *Human Migration: Patterns and Policies* (Indiana University Press, 1979), p. 61.

burdened with the rising aspirations of their nationals for improved economic opportunities.

There is no way to determine what proportion of current immigration is the product of political forces or even to distinguish clearly between political and economic forces. The debate about whether Haitians who flee their country and seek refuge here are motivated by political or economic considerations illustrates the problem. Undoubtedly many people emigrate because they are unhappy with the political regime under which they live; some may feel that their lives or freedoms are threatened by the regime or they may feel uneasy because of political unrest, while others may experience direct political pressures to leave their homelands. This category would include the Jews migrating from the Soviet Union in recent years, the thousands of immigrants arriving from Central and South America and from the Caribbean, and the hundreds of thousands of refugees admitted to the United States since the early 1960s.

Civil strife in its neighboring countries has helped to increase migration to the United States. For example, the assassination in 1961 of President Rafael Trujillo, the dictator who had ruled the Dominican Republic for thirty-one years, precipitated several years of civil strife during which both legal and illegal immigration from the Dominican Republic increased sharply. The political turmoil in Colombia during the 1960s also spurred migration to this country. Similarly, the current strife in El Salvador, Nicaragua, and Guatemala has prompted thousands of people there to flee to the United States as routine immigrants, nonimmigrants, or illegal immigrants entering via Mexico.

Political forces are among the principal causes of refugee flows. Although some refugees leave their homelands because of natural disasters, the overwhelming majority of the approximately 15 million refugees around the world left because of political factors, as did virtually all of the nearly 2 million admitted to this country since 1946. Many were uprooted or displaced by wars and the accompanying realignment of national boundaries. Others, like the Cubans and Indochinese, fled from newly installed political regimes to which they were opposed or were forced out by these regimes.

A slightly different case is that of the several thousand Haitians who have made their way by boat to the Florida coast since 1979. The federal government has not recognized these people as political refugees, arguing instead that they are mainly victims of prolonged drought, famine, and severe economic hardships. However, these Haitians left a political regime widely viewed as oppressive and abusive to its nationals, and they and many observers claim that their flight was precipitated by their fear of that regime. These conflicting views of their reasons for leaving and, in the view of some, their race, have led the federal government to resist admitting them as refugees.

Another factor to influence the flow of immigrants since 1945 has been communist expansion. The establishment of communist regimes in several eastern European countries and the subsequent flight of large numbers of their nationals led the United States to define the refugee status as synonymous with flight from communism. Its admission of such refugees became an important part of the country's struggle against communism. The massive influx of Cuban refugees after Fidel Castro's rise to power was accompanied by the same anticommunist themes associated with the earlier admission of refugees from eastern Europe and the Soviet Union. The direct U.S. military involvement in Vietnam made the influx of Indochinese refugees somewhat different from the other large-scale refugee admissions in that this involvement imposed a special obligation on the country. However, the fact that the refugees were fleeing from communist regimes undoubtedly contributed to the government's willingness to admit them and to the sympathetic reception they received from the public. In all of these instances the politics of anticommunism was at least as strong a force behind refugee admission as were the country's humanitarian concerns.

Like the economic push forces, political conditions around

the world are likely to continue to generate large streams of immigrants. Their numbers are already high, as Deputy Secretary of State Warren Christopher pointed out to a meeting of the Permanent Council of the Organization of American States in July 1980; commenting on the approximately 15 million refugees and displaced persons around the world then, Christopher declared, "Ours is becoming an epoch of refugees."[30]

Although most of these refugees will probably return to their home countries, many cannot do so safely and will have to be resettled or kept indefinitely in makeshift refugee camps. Several hundred thousand will enter the United States. They are almost sure to be joined by many more who will be forced to flee as the result of other conflicts within or between countries. Because of U.S. involvement in areas of the world experiencing major political upheavals, the American public—aided by modern communication systems—has become more aware of the plight of refugees than at any time since the end of World War II. Its concern has generated further pressure to admit refugees.

The Pull of the United States

Regardless of the circumstances under which they came, immigrants have been—and continue to be—attracted to this country primarily because of two factors. One is greater economic opportunity—availability of jobs, higher wages, greater access to arable land, or greater opportunity for entrepreneurship than in their homelands. The other is the relatively hospitable social and political climate of the United States.

The American Labor Market

Employment at relatively high wages has been by far the most powerful of the forces to draw immigrants to the United

30. Warren Christopher, *Refugees: A Global Issue*, prepared for the U.S. Department of State, Current Policy Series, 201 (July 23, 1980), p. 1.

States, most of them from countries with inadequate employment opportunities and low wages. The U.S. immigration
experience is certainly not unique in this regard since most of
the world's migration flows have been stimulated by the need
for workers and their search for jobs. Some analysts have
questioned whether it is the pull of the labor market or the
push of economic hardship at home that is the primary force
in the migration decision. Undoubtedly the two interact to
produce immigration.

Stressing the role of the pull of the economy, some have
noted that immigration tends to rise and fall in response to
expansions and contractions in business activity and therefore
in employment opportunities. Where business is expanding
and the country is experiencing rapid economic growth, immigrants come in growing numbers to take a share of the
increasing wages and employment. On the other hand, during
business depressions their numbers decline sharply. Others
have suggested that the pull of the U.S. labor market is in turn
related to broad structural features of the international system.
One such hypothesis is that in the international capitalist
system a powerful and highly developed country like the
United States can create and maintain dependency relationships
with poorer, less developed countries on its periphery and that
this relationship determines the movement of workers from
the periphery to the center.[31] Still another view is that the
United States, like all developed capitalist countries, has a two-
tiered or dual labor market in which domestic workers are
constantly seeking to move from the low-wage jobs in the
lower tier to the better-paying and more prestigious jobs in the
top tier, with the result that immigrants are called upon to fill
the jobs in the lower tier.[32]

These perspectives call attention to important elements of

31. Alejandro Portes, "Toward a Structural Analysis of Illegal (Undocumented)
Immigration," *International Migration Review*, vol. 12 (Winter 1978), p. 472.

32. Michael Piore, *Birds of Passage: Migrant Labor and Industrial Societies* (New York:
Cambridge University Press, 1979), pp. 35–43.

the country's immigration experience. That is to say, foreign nationals have been attracted to the U.S. labor market not only because of general reports about the economic opportunities here or the advice of relatives and friends already here, but also because of the direct efforts of employers and the U.S. government. At times the flow of immigrants allowed by law has not been adequate to meet labor force demands so that the federal government has turned to temporary workers to augment the labor force. Temporary work programs have been in use since at least 1942 and they have brought in workers from Canada, the Caribbean countries, and Mexico, mostly for agricultural jobs.[33]

The pull of the American labor market has probably been strongest for Mexicans. For decades they crossed the border without authorization and without much hindrance, providing the agricultural sector with an abundant supply of inexpensive labor. Many also worked in factories and more recently in this country's expanding urban service industries. When the flow failed to subside in response to a declining labor demand in the 1970s, the U.S. government attempted to curtail it through stepped-up enforcement of immigration laws and through new legislation. The Simpson-Mazzoli bill sought to achieve this curtailment. Yet, reflecting the country's continued need for immigrant workers, it provided for the admission of up to 500,000 temporary workers annually in an expanded temporary worker program.

The Political and Social Climate

The "American way of life" has also drawn many immigrants to this country. Although no standard definition of this phrase exists, it generally refers to the relatively high level of social and political freedom enjoyed by individuals in this country

33. See Edwin P. Reubens, *Temporary Admission of Foreign Workers: Dimensions and Policies*, Special Report, 34 (Washington, D.C.: National Commission for Manpower Policy, 1979), pp. 12–17.

and to the opportunities for individual achievement. Early in the country's history, when national leaders sought to encourage immigration, they made a point of advertising the religious and political freedom the country offered. The country has remained a social and political haven, one that has become especially important to the people of the non-European developing countries whose still-fragile political systems are in many cases not yet able to guarantee basic individual rights and freedoms.

The communications revolution that has occurred since 1950 has undoubtedly strengthened the appeal of the United States by making its values and standard of living known to the entire world through radio, television, and motion pictures. At the same time the United States itself has publicized the American way of life abroad and extolled its virtues as the virtues of the capitalist system in the global postwar propaganda contest with communism. Immigrants have been able to respond to these forces because of the relative ease with which people can move around the world. More people from more countries now travel to the United States than at any time in its history. Coming as temporary workers, tourists, or students, people of the developing countries have become familiar with U.S. society and undoubtedly have disseminated information about it within their societies. Between 1965 and 1980 travel to the United States, measured by the total number of visas issued annually, increased almost fivefold (see chapter 4). The rate of increase in travel from developing countries was especially high.

The quality of life or standard of living in the United States now far exceeds that of the developing countries, as can be seen from the differences in the physical quality of life index (PQLI) for these countries.[34] The PQLI was developed by the Overseas Development Council as a means of measuring the extent to which all the people of a country benefit from essential goods and services that make for good health and education.

34. Morris David Morris, *Measuring the Conditions of the World's Poor* (Pergamon Press, 1979), app. A.

It is based on vital statistics that are available for most countries—a baby's life expectancy at age one, the infant mortality rate, and the literacy rate. These three measures are believed to reflect educational levels, nutritional levels, availability of safe water, public health services, medical care, and the levels of other services used to satisfy basic human needs.

Most of the countries that are principal sources of illegal immigration have quality of life conditions that are drastically below those of the United States.[35] Not surprisingly, as information about the standard of living in the United States spreads throughout these developing countries and as aspirations rise, efforts to migrate to the United States can be expected to rise or at least remain at their current high levels.

The Facilitating Conditions

Most developing countries experience the push-pull pressures that have been identified here. That only a small number of people actually attempt to immigrate suggests that other factors must be present before the dissatisfied and aspiring individual is transformed into an immigrant. At least four of these facilitating factors appear to be especially important: a migrant-supportive culture; proximity to the United States; the presence of a familiar national or ethnic community in the United States; and, for illegal immigrants, relatively easy access to the country without inspection.

Migrant-Supportive Cultures

Before an individual's discontent or frustration at home produces the inclination to emigrate, that individual must come to perceive emigration as a legitimate or appropriate course. Such a perception is more likely to develop in a society that readily accepts or encourages migration—in other words, one

35. Ibid.

that has a migrant tradition. Interestingly enough, that is the case for most of the countries that are principal sources of immigration in the world today.

Mexico, the largest source of immigration to the United States, has a migrant tradition of long standing. Internal strife, the desire for adventure, and the search for work turned Mexicans into a highly mobile people well before the current borders with the United States were established. For decades afterward they continued to migrate to the United States periodically, to search for work or to escape domestic turmoil. Labor shortages in the United States during the war years of the 1940s contributed considerably to this inclination to emigrate because Mexican workers were actually recruited by the U.S. government and private employers in this country.

Another significant factor is the brisk internal migration that took place after 1940 as scores left the countryside for Mexico City and other major cities. By the second half of the 1940s, the Mexican government took steps to increase agricultural productivity, but these measures merely accelerated the migration from rural areas to cities, especially to those on the northern border. In 1940 only about one-third of Mexico's population lived in urban areas (places with a population of 2,500 or more), but by 1980 two-thirds of the population lived in these areas, the northern border cities being among the fastest growing.[36]

Migration has been part of the way of life in the Caribbean basin countries as well. For more than a century people have migrated within the region and outside it, largely in search of employment. They found it in Cuba, first on the sugar plantations and in the sugar factories there, and more recently on the Guantanamo military base, where they have participated in its construction and maintenance; in Panama, where they helped to construct the canal; and in the United States, on

36. Lourdes Arizpe, "The Rural Exodus in Mexico and Mexican Migration to the United States," in Peter G. Brown and Henry Shue, eds., *The Border That Joins: Mexican Migrants and U.S. Responsibility* (Totowa, N.J.: Roman and Littlefield, 1983), p. 180.

farms and in factories. In addition, thousands of migrants from the British colonies in the Caribbean traveled to the United Kingdom (some also came to this country) in response to labor shortages during both world wars. By 1960–62 migration from the English-speaking Caribbean countries to the United Kingdom had reached an all-time high.[37] However, the United Kingdom drastically curtailed this flow by imposing restrictions on non-Caucasian Commonwealth countries in the Commonwealth Immigration Act of 1962.[38] After the island countries won their independence and the United States and Canada eliminated the racially and ethnically discriminatory features of their immigration laws in 1965, the flow from the Caribbean to these countries increased rapidly, becoming one of the major streams.

The early 1960s also saw large-scale emigration in several South American countries. Many of the immigrants came to the United States, but some moved to other countries within the continent. Migrants from Colombia crossed into Venezuela (and still do so) in much the same way that Mexicans have been migrating to this country illegally. Other smaller, long-established streams, such as that from Uruguay to Argentina, have also persisted.

Without doubt, emigration is a widely accepted path to economic or professional advancement in these countries and several others. It provides opportunities for those who choose to reside here permanently or who decide to earn relatively large amounts of money with which they can improve their status when they return home. The governments of many of these countries see migration as a valuable opportunity for their nationals and sometimes intervene with the governments of receiving countries to ensure or to increase the flow.

---

37. *Undocumented Workers: Implications for U.S. Policy in the Western Hemisphere*, prepared for the Subcommittee on Inter-American Affairs of the House International Relations Committee, 95 Cong. 2 sess. (GPO, 1978), pp. 51–61, 215–25.

38. Dawn Marshall, "Toward an Understanding of Caribbean Migration," in Kritz, ed., *U.S. Immigration and Refugee Policy*, pp. 121–22.

Ease of Access

One of the most important facilitating conditions for immigrants is that they be able to enter a country without great expense or difficulty. Ease of access is afforded by proximity, a relatively open border, a liberal visa policy, and an established network of smugglers, guides, and other middlemen to facilitate surreptitious or fraudulent entry by those unable to qualify for admission or unwilling to try. The importance of proximity is attested to by the fact that five of the top ten source countries for legal immigration to the United States and nine of the top ten for illegal immigration are nearby countries. Proximity reduces the cost of immigration and thus the risk to illegal immigrants for whom immigration is an investment; it also makes overland travel possible for some, and ensures that relatively accurate information about the United States and the opportunities there will be available.

One of the notable features of this country's immigration experience is the ease of access across the land borders. The federal government's weak efforts to control the land border in the past and the apparently large number of smugglers and guides involved in effecting surreptitious entries have made it easy for large numbers of Mexicans and nationals of nearby Central American countries to enter this country. Although the pressures for entry have not been as great on the northern border, access there has been equally easy and extensively exploited.

Ethnic and Nationality Ties in the United States

Still another facilitating factor is the existence of ethnic communities or "ethnic enclaves" that serve as information channels about employment opportunities and living conditions in the host country. Such enclaves also provide a friendly, familiar, and supportive environment for newcomers and reduce the risk and trauma of illegal residence for some.

This, of course, has been the traditional role of the ethnic or nationality communities, but some have also been part of a highly organized and financially rewarding system in which certain members of the ethnic community, as in the case of the "padrone" system of an earlier era, for a fee recruited fellow nationals from their hometown and helped them to emigrate.[39] The settlement patterns of new immigrants indicate that similar systems are in operation today; most new arrivals settle in urban centers where ethnic communities are already well established, thereby recreating the ethnic mosaic characteristic of many cities in the United States during earlier phases of immigration.

Mexican aliens, for example, especially deportable ones, have settled primarily in the Southwest and in a few midwestern cities where long-established ethnic bases are present. The pull of long-established communities is also evident in the concentration of West Indians in sections of New York City, in Miami, and in a few other cities along the eastern seaboard; the Asians and Indochinese in California; or the concentration of Cubans in Dade Country, Florida, and Hudson County, New Jersey. Even though most Indochinese were deliberately dispersed in the resettlement process, they too have established major enclaves in Pacific gateway cities like Los Angeles and San Francisco.

Strong ethnic or nationality ties and the proximity of the source country mean, first, that immigrants are by no means strangers who are invading the United States in an unordered mass, but that they are participants in a long tradition that is being perpetuated, often in spite of laws that attempt to restrict it. Moreover, these ethnic communities may be an important factor in making immigration, at least from the Western Hemisphere, an instrument of regional integration. Although the attitudes of Western Hemisphere immigrants toward the United States have not been extensively studied, the general view

39. See, for example, Robert F. Foerster, *The Italian Emigration of Our Times* (Harvard University Press, 1919), pp. 326–27.

appears to be that cities like New York and Miami are extensions of home metropolitan areas. If that is the case, immigrants serve as a strong link between the United States and the major source countries. At the same time, these connections will likely make it difficult for this country to control the flow of immigration by means of administrative actions.

How Controllable Is Immigration?

The trends described here and the forces behind them raise three fundamental questions for policymakers seeking to reform immigration policy: How appropriate is the current number and mix of immigrants? What attention should be given to the needs of source countries in immigration policy decisions? And, to what extent can policy decisions or administrative efforts actually control immigration? In one form or another these issues have been at the heart of the country's century-long struggle with immigration policy.

The question of number and mix has been easily the most controversial and the most basic one in immigration policy, raising as it does the full range of conflicting sentiments that have produced this country's ambivalence about immigration. Many of these sentiments in turn have been evoked by the complex array of costs and benefits that immigration produces and their uneven distribution throughout the population. Not surprisingly, policymakers have relied on the clash of competing interests to yield answers to the question of number and mix instead of attempting to ascertain empirically what might be most appropriate.

What constitutes an appropriate level of immigration will be difficult to determine in the absence of clear criteria. The most widely used criteria thus far have been population growth rates and labor market effects, but unless the country develops a national growth policy that specifies a desirable rate of population growth and people can agree about how immigration affects the domestic labor market, neither of these criteria will be very helpful. Some observers consider any significant level of population growth a threat to the quality of life and therefore urge highly restrictive immigration policies, whereas others are undisturbed by modest growth rates and therefore support less restrictive policies. Views about the effects of immigration on the labor market are just as divergent. Some analysts, as mentioned earlier, believe that immigrants displace domestic workers and depress wages, whereas others believe that they stimulate economic activity and therefore help to expand employment opportunities.

The level of immigration legislated is likely to continue to represent political compromises, while assertions about the country's "maximum absorptive capacity" are likely to remain decorative phrases. The compromises up to now have been extremely conservative, but perhaps the country should consider prescribing a level much closer to the actual level of total immigration, since that level probably reflects the country's real needs more than the politically derived ceilings now do. Ceilings that ignore the country's demand for immigrants or the external pressures that push them will almost certainly impose an unrealistic enforcement burden on the government. Indeed, current illegal immigration might be at least partly a product of this problem.

Although the interests of the United States must be paramount in the formulation of immigration policy, immigration is inherently an international phenomenon and domestic policy decisions can have far-reaching effects on other countries. Not only do circumstances in source countries (the push forces) play as great a role in the process as the needs and preferences of this country, many of the source countries now rely heavily on the benefits that accrue from the migration of their nationals. Moreover, immigration can be a means of addressing some of this country's foreign policy interests. This notion is generally accepted in the formulation of refugee policies, but it tends to be overlooked in decisions about other forms of immigration.

A growing number of analysts and public officials are now suggesting that the United States should assist the principal source countries with the social and economic problems that push their nationals to this country. These problems are complex and are mounting rapidly, but few if any of the countries have the resources to tackle them effectively. Even Mexico, which does have vast energy resources, has been unable to significantly improve economic opportunities for its burgeoning population and, according to some analysts, it is unlikely to do so if its current policies are maintained.

The political outlook globally is no better than the economic one to the extent that the two are even separable. Political turmoil and instability are growing, and there is little reason to believe that substantial improvement will occur soon. These conditions suggest that refugee flows or other forms of politically motivated immigration are likely to remain at their current high levels or even rise higher.

In addition to producing strong pressures for admission, these conditions are adding new dimensions to the country's immigrant experience. Most notable is that the United States has become a place of "first asylum" for thousands of refugees such as the Haitian boat people and the refugees from conflicts in several Central American countries. Before these developments took place, the United States was able to decide whether to admit a particular refugee population, how many it would admit, and at what pace. As a country of first asylum it loses these choices. Its reaction to this development thus far, which is embarrassingly far removed from the values and principles it has espoused, has been to detain and seek to expel most of the Haitians and to refuse to accord refugee status to Salvadoran and Nicaraguan nationals who come here to escape the violence at home.

Admittedly, efforts must be made to address these push forces, but it is not entirely clear what specific actions might be undertaken or how effective they would be. Possibilities frequently suggested are: (1) increased trade concessions to enable at least Mexico and the Caribbean basin countries to market more of their products here; (2) financial and technical assistance for rural development and improved agricultural productivity; and (3) population planning assistance. Although these actions would focus on primary areas of need, enormous sums and considerable time would be required to achieve significant results from any or all of them. Moreover, measures such as trade concessions would encounter stiff opposition from workers and business people likely to be adversely affected by them. For many of the countries, the most direct and effective form of assistance might well be the opportunities for their nationals to emigrate.

The complexity of immigration issues and the power of the forces that produce immigration make it highly unlikely that legislation can fully control immigration. Historically, the mix of immigrants never quite conformed to the preferences legislated; and currently the level of immigration far exceeds the legislated ceilings.

The policy problem is certainly not confined to illegal immigration. The 1980 Refugee Act, which attempted to delineate national refugee policy and procedure, had just become law when the sudden Mariel boatlift brought in thousands of Cubans and scores of other boats brought the Haitians, all without prior authorization and seeking refuge. These developments were not anticipated by the refugee law and posed formidable policy and administrative problems for the federal government as well as the affected localities. The influx of Cuban and Haitian boat people has quickly brought to light further issues that are yet to be resolved in dealing with claims for refuge.

It is unlikely that immigration policy as now devised will ever be entirely effective in controlling immigration. One reason is that the phenomenon is simply not susceptible to complete control by one country alone—either the sending or receiving country—particularly in situations where immigration pressures are very strong. Another is that U.S. immigration policy glosses over a number of specific issues on which a consensus among policymakers cannot be reached. Furthermore, effective control of immigration requires policies that go well beyond the elements that now make up immigration policy. For example, policies having to do with foreign aid and trade, wage and hour standards, and other labor standards are all inextricably linked with immigration, but the manner of policy-making makes it virtually impossible to consider these together. Thus, although policy decisions determine the overall pattern of immigration and to a great extent the basic levels of immigration and the composition of the immigrant streams, much will depend on the effective integration of several related policies and on the effective administration of these policies.

4

Administering Immigration Policies

FORMULATING adequate immigration policies is one side of the effort to control immigration; administering those policies is the other. This task is currently shared by six agencies of the federal government, two of which have the primary responsibility for enforcement—the Justice Department's Immigration and Naturalization Service (INS) within the country, and the State Department's Bureau of Consular Affairs outside it.[1] The other agencies that deal with immigration matters are the Office of Labor Certification in the Department of Labor, the Bureau of Public Health and the Office of Refugee Resettlement in the Department of Health and Human Services, and the Office of the U.S. Coordinator for Refugee Affairs in the Executive Office of the President.

The Beleaguered Immigration Bureaucracy

In recent years, few agencies of the federal government have been as vigorously or persistently criticized as those engaged in enforcing immigration policy. The INS in particular has been

1. The principal responsibility of the bureau is the issuance of visas, which is administered by the bureau's visa office.

a target of widespread criticism, even among public officials. Testifying before a House Appropriations Subcommittee in 1977, Representative Joshua Eilberg, Democrat of Pennsylvania, chairman of the Subcommittee on Immigration, Naturalization, and International Law of the House Judiciary Committee, declared that "the INS at the present time is totally incapable of administering and enforcing provisions of the Immigration and Nationality Act."[2] His successor to the chairmanship of the subcommittee, Representative Elizabeth Holtzman, Democrat of New York, commented in 1979 that the INS "still uses 19th century tools," has "a record-keeping system that is a disaster," and generally lacks professionalism.[3] Other members of Congress, journalists, and several General Accounting Office (GAO) reports have all painted a similarly grim picture of the agency—showing it to be inadequately equipped, overwhelmed by its work, deeply demoralized, and in a hopeless state of disarray.[4]

Although the Bureau of Consular Affairs has received considerably less public criticism than the INS, it too is problem-ridden. Several consular posts abroad are inadequately staffed to promptly process requests for U.S. visas. Applicants, therefore, are often forced to wait in long lines in applying for a visa and to wait a long time to have the applications processed. Moreover, many people in this country fear that because too few people spend too little time reviewing visa applications, the incidence of visa abuse is much higher than it would be otherwise.

The inadequacies of the two principal units of the immigra-

2. *Departments of State, Justice, and Commerce, the Judiciary, and Related Agencies Appropriations for 1978*, Hearings before the Subcommittee on State, Justice and Commerce, and the Judiciary of the House Appropriations Committee, 95 Cong. 1 sess. (Government Printing Office, 1977), pt. 7, p. 444.

3. Quoted in Bernard Weinraub, "Immigration Bureaucracy Is Overwhelmed by Its Work," *New York Times*, January 17, 1980.

4. See General Accounting Office, *Need for Improvement in Management Activities of INS* (GAO, 1977); and *Prospects Dim for Effectively Enforcing Immigration Laws* (GAO, 1980). Also see "The Great American Immigration Nightmare," *U.S. News & World Report* (June 22, 1981), pp. 27–32.

tion bureaucracy are reflected in the mounting evidence of large-scale illegal immigration, in the frequent failure of the bureaucracy to provide certain routine services effectively and expeditiously, and in its inability to maintain and provide routine immigration data on demand. Some of these failings are no doubt the result of normal organizational or management problems experienced by virtually all agencies of government. Overall, however, they appear to stem from serious structural problems within the immigration bureaucracy, and from the way it approaches its administrative responsibilities.

This beleaguered immigration bureaucracy is a troubling symbol of the country's vulnerability to the mounting pressures for immigration described in chapter 3 and of its long-standing ambivalence about immigration. The ambivalence has led to serious and sometimes immobilizing conflicts in which the desire to impose firm and, to some, draconian enforcement measures has come up against the desire to preserve the society's cherished values of openness to immigrants and respect for individual rights. This situation has contributed to the government's casual approach to enforcement, the fragmented character of the immigration bureaucracy, and the lack of clear and consistent enforcement objectives.

Inadequate Government Attention to Enforcement

Before 1876 the federal government had little to do with administering immigration laws. The necessary administrative tasks, such as enumerating and admitting immigrants and collecting a head tax from them, were carried out by the governments of states where immigrants disembarked. At the time some people considered this a much more efficient arrangement than having the federal government carry out these tasks because, as one observer argued, assigning this responsibility to

the clumsy machinery of a central board, or . . . a single Commissioner stationed at an inland city, remote from the chief objective points of foreign immigration, with an unwieldy multitude of subordinates scattered over the land . . . would be worse than unreasonable. The transfer to the national government of the control of the immigrant would lead to quarrels, heart-burnings.[5]

However, in 1876 the Supreme Court invalidated the laws of California, New York, and Louisiana that regulated various aspects of immigration, and thereby placed full responsibility for immigration matters on the federal government.

In response to this judicial action and to the enactment of several immigration laws shortly thereafter, a federal administrative apparatus gradually developed. The nucleus of that apparatus was the Treasury Department's Bureau of Immigration, which had been established in July 1891 pursuant to the Immigration Act of that year. Other immigration laws not only added new responsibilities to that bureau but also shifted it from one department to another until it finally came to reside in the Justice Department as the INS. However, federal policymakers took little notice of whether the INS was able to carry out the tasks assigned to it, despite the complaints of immigration bureau officials themselves, who since the early 1900s have consistently underscored the problems of inadequate staff, funds, and facilities—obviously with little effect. As the number of aliens entering the country and the enforcement responsibilities increased, these problems worsened and in 1919 reached a point where the Commissioner General for Immigration was led to complain:

As immigration laws have been extended more and more into new fields and as their restrictive features have become more stringent, making it more difficult for the inadmissible classes to enter the United States, so there have been added greater responsibilities and a vast amount of labor not before usual in the bureau's administrative work. Thus, the bureau has made recommendations for additions to its legal staff and other sub-

5. Friedrich Kapp, *Immigration and the Commissioners of Emigration* (Arno Press, 1969), p. 155.

divisions, which it considers absolutely necessary to meet the growing business and responsibilities that rest upon it.[6]

Sixty years later almost the same complaint was raised by acting INS Commissioner David Crosland in his 1979 testimony on the service's budget request:

> Major changes in the law in 1965 resulted in considerably more paperwork for the Agency, and it was not and has not been equipped to cope with it, either through systems and procedures or through automation. At the same time immigration to this country has been increasing substantially and we now find ourselves in a hole from which it will not be easy to extricate ourselves.[7]

In 1979, as in 1919, federal policymakers acknowledged the problem but did nothing about it. In short, neither Congress nor the executive branch has shown much willingness to tackle the administrative problems that have afflicted the immigration bureaucracy, particularly the INS.

Fragmented Administrative Structure

One of the distinctive features of the immigration bureau-cracy is its fragmented structure—it consists of six major units spread across four departments and the Office of the President. The bureaucracy developed in this way because of the manner in which the administrative responsibilities evolved and be-cause immigration affairs have both domestic and international dimensions. From the beginning new administrative tasks were assigned to the existing agency or department that appeared best equipped at the time to carry out the task. The division of responsibilities in this way has impeded the enforcement effort somewhat, because cooperation, communication, and

6. Quoted in *History of the Immigration and Naturalization Service*, prepared for the Select Commission on Immigration and Refugee Policy, 96 Cong. 2 sess. (GPO, 1980), p. 25.

7. *State, Justice, Commerce, the Judiciary, and Related Agencies Appropriations, Fiscal Year 1981*, Hearings before the Senate Committee on Appropriations, 96 Cong. 2 sess. (GPO, 1980), pt. 2, p. 740.

collaboration among the separate enforcement entities have been difficult to achieve. In recent years communication between the INS and the Bureau of Consular Affairs has improved, but that is due mainly to the strong efforts of the principal officials on both sides.

Divided up as it is, the immigration bureaucracy lacks the stature within the federal government that would allow it to compete effectively for the resources it needs to carry out its responsibilities. Both the INS and the Bureau of Consular Affairs are relatively weak agencies of their respective departments. Many observers have noted the relatively low status of the INS, which is headed by a commissioner who does not even report directly to the attorney general, and on its remoteness from the Justice Department's primary activities. The Bureau of Consular Affairs has a similar problem; the consular service, especially visa responsibilities, has not been viewed by foreign service officers as a highly desirable foreign service assignment, and visa issuance is well removed from the State Department's principal activities.

Lack of Clear Objectives

Because the government's objectives with respect to the enforcement of immigration policy are varied and sometimes contradictory, the work of the immigration bureaucracy is considerably more difficult than it might otherwise be. Although this problem was recognized as long ago as 1903 in the annual report of the Bureau of Immigration, little has been done to change the situation.[8] Instead immigration policy has evolved to reflect a wide array of competing interests, and in consequence enforcement responsibilities have multiplied and central purposes have become blurred.

What has happened can be seen in broad terms in the policy requiring visa applicants to be thoroughly screened. Only those who qualify under existing law are to be admitted; those whose presence would adversely affect the domestic work force are

8. *History of the Immigration and Naturalization Service,* p. 12.

to be excluded; unauthorized or clandestine entry is to be prevented; and aliens who violate immigration laws are to be apprehended and expelled or otherwise penalized. In the management of immigration across the land borders, especially the southern border, however, policy has had to yield to the demographic, geographic, political, and economic realities of the region. As a result, some illegal entries have been allowed and even encouraged at times for many years and often a less than vigorous effort has been made to apprehend and expel those who enter the country illegally across the southern border.

A case of such encouragement or tolerance can be found in the "drying out of wetbacks" that occurred in the Southwest during the 1940s and 1950s. "Drying out" meant conferring legal status on Mexicans working in this country illegally. The practice by INS personnel began in 1926 as a means of placating growers in the Imperial Valley of California, whose supply of Mexican workers was interrupted by the restrictive immigration law of 1924.[9] Although it was clearly a violation of immigration law, the practice continued into the 1940s even when the bracero or temporary worker program was in effect and allowed Mexicans to contract for work in the United States. In addition, the U.S. Border Patrol sometimes assisted the growers by simply failing to act forcefully to prevent unauthorized entries. Thus, INS enforcement practices at the southern border often were at variance with the country's overall policy.

Such conflicts exist even in the routine screening of foreign nationals wanting to enter the country as tourists. For example, the United States has increasingly emphasized that tourism contributes sizably to its economy. To facilitate tourism, public agencies and private organizations have tried to speed up and simplify the admission process. The immigration bureaucracy, meanwhile, is required to screen all applicants for admission thoroughly, but in doing so it risks slowing down the flow of tourists.

As might be expected from the way in which it operates,

9. Mark Reigler, *By the Sweat of Their Brow: Mexican Immigrant Labor in the United States, 1900–1940* (Greenwood Press, 1976), p. 61.

the beleaguered immigration bureaucracy faces other major problems that affect the country's ability to control immigration. They show up primarily in four types of administrative tasks: (1) managing the flow of aliens into the country; (2) ensuring that aliens within the country comply with immigration laws; (3) providing immigration-related services to the public in this country and abroad; and (4) resettling refugees.

Managing the Flow of Aliens

The immigration bureaucracy's most important responsibility is to manage the flow of aliens into the country. Before 1917 flow management amounted to minimal screening of aliens seeking admission at ports of entry to ensure that they met the health and character qualifications established by law. However, the task became much more laborious when in July 1917 the federal government instituted a requirement that all immigrants would have to be screened and issued visas in their home country before traveling to a U.S. port of entry. Flow management now encompasses some other activities as well: the inspection of aliens at the port of entry (so as to prevent fraudulent or mala fide entry), the prevention of clandestine entries away from official entry points, and the screening and admitting of refugees. Each of these tasks has become increasingly demanding as the overall number of aliens seeking admission to the country has increased.

Visa Issuance

The visa requirement has become the principal means of managing the flow of aliens into the country. All aliens traveling to the United States are required to have an entry visa with the exception of Canadian citizens who are temporary visitors and a few others in that category. This general visa requirement, first established by a joint order of the secretaries of labor and state in July 1917 and enacted into law in May 1918, was introduced primarily as a national security measure. With the imposition of annual ceilings on total immigration and quotas for each country in 1921 and the introduction of a preference system in 1952 whereby visas are distributed among several types or categories of immigrants, visa issuance has grown quite complicated.

Numerical limitations apply only to immigrant visas. Individuals may enter the country on nonimmigrant visas for business, pleasure, study, or diplomatic purposes, or they can be here in transit, provided they meet certain standards established by immigration law. The basic conditions are that applicants for nonimmigrant visas must have a bona fide reason for traveling to the United States; be able to support themselves while they are in the country; evidence a clear intention to depart upon expiration of the authorized stay; and meet certain health, character, and national security criteria.

Immigrant visas, on the other hand, are subject to a number of restrictions. First, under current law, only 270,000 immigrant visas can be issued annually, not including 50,000 refugee visas. Spouses, parents, and children of adult U.S. citizens and a few other categories of aliens are also admitted outside this ceiling. Next, each country is allocated no more than 20,000 of the numerically restricted visas annually. Finally, immigration law establishes a system of six preferences under which applicants for immigrant visas are classified, four based on family ties to residents of the United States and two on employment-related expertise or special skills needed in this country (see table 3-1). Immigrants must also meet basic health, character, and national security criteria and they must demonstrate that their resources or those of a sponsor are enough to ensure that they will not become a financial burden to the government, in other words, a public charge, for at least five years after entry.[10]

U.S. consular officials stationed abroad are responsible for

10. Immigration and Nationality Act, 8 U.S.C. 1101 et. seq. For the law as amended through September 1, 1980, see *Immigration and Nationality Act with Amendments and Notes on Related Laws*, Committee Print, prepared for the House Committee on the Judiciary, 96 Cong. 2. sess. (GPO, 1980).

screening visa applicants and for issuing visas to those who qualify. Although immigration law specifies the qualifications for admission, consular officers are ordinarily the final arbiters of whether an individual meets these qualifications. For example, the consular officer must judge whether an applicant for an immigrant visa who is otherwise eligible is able to be self-supporting in the United States, or whether an applicant for a nonimmigrant visa has a legitimate reason for wanting to travel to the United States but also strong enough ties to his or her home country to ensure return.

The Department of Labor's Office of Labor Certification participates in the screening of one small category of immigrants, those admitted under the sixth preference to accept employment offered by a U.S. employer. That office must find that there are no local workers qualified, willing, and available to take the job the applicant plans to take, whereupon the secretary of labor must grant a labor certification before a visa is issued.

Visa issuance has become increasingly demanding as the number of applications has increased. The increase in the number of immigrant visas issued has been modest, only about 13 percent, between 1972 and 1980—from 293,966 to 331,345 (see table 4-1). (Visas issued in a year often do not equal immigrants admitted for that year.) However, the number of applications has been growing more rapidly, resulting in a mounting backlog that exceeded 1.4 million in January 1983, according to the deputy assistant secretary of state for visa affairs.[11] Nonimmigrant visas issued during 1972–80 almost tripled in number, going from 2.29 million to 6.73 million (table 4-1). As a result, consular officials have much less time to examine applications and ferret out fraudulent or otherwise unqualified applicants. (Consular officials are said to spend an

---

11. U.S. Department of State, speech by the deputy assistant secretary for visa services to the 1983 annual conference of the American Immigration Lawyers Association.

Table 4-1. *Immigrant and Nonimmigrant Visas Issued by the United States, 1965–80*

Year	Immigrant visas	Nonimmigrant visas	Total
1965	280,212	1,173,149	1,453,361
1966	289,472	1,256,751	1,546,223
1967	294,250	1,443,786	1,738,036
1968	349,468	1,538,070	1,887,538
1969	313,632	1,759,608	2,073,240
1970	309,701	2,039,569	2,349,270
1971	296,500	2,148,901	2,445,401
1972	293,966	2,290,576	2,584,542
1973	304,758	2,834,152	3,138,910
1974	321,136	3,156,293	3,477,429
1975	302,604	3,353,497	3,656,101
1976	310,364	3,683,533	3,993,897
1977	330,192	3,874,666	4,204,858
1978	364,330	4,727,312	5,091,642
1979	315,684	5,894,959	6,210,643
1980	331,345	6,728,732	7,060,077

Sources: For 1965–76, U.S. Department of State, Bureau of Security and Consular Affairs, *Report of the Visa Office*, various years, p. 3. For 1976–80, provided by Bureau of Consular Affairs in "Monthly Workload Reports" and "Semi-Annual Reports of Non-immigrant Visas Issued and Refused."

average of about two minutes or less per nonimmigrant visa applicant.)[12]

Among nonimmigrants, tourists account for the majority of visas issued and for most of the increase during 1972–80, which no doubt occurred in response to the vigorous promotion of tourism by the U.S. government and the private sector. Reductions in the relative cost of living in this country and readily available and inexpensive transportation have made U.S. vacations attractive to increasing numbers of people. The number of visa issuances for foreign students coming here each year to study also has increased sharply, from 65,750 in fiscal year 1972 to 154,960 in fiscal year 1980.[13]

Beside having to cope with the problem of sheer numbers,

12. Sidney L. Smith, *Nonimmigrant Visa Processing at U.S. Consulate General, Toronto*, Technical Report M78-210 (Bedford, Mass.: Mitre Corp., 1977), p. iii. The time spent per visa applicant varies among consular offices.
13. U.S. Department of State, Bureau of Consular Affairs, *1972 and 1980 Report of the Visa Office*, table 19.

visa officials must contend with fraud or misrepresentation in visa applications. Although the extent of fraud in visa petitions is unknown, there is some evidence to suggest that it is a substantial problem, but that it is confined to a relatively small number of visa posts, most of them in developing countries where the pressures for emigration are especially strong. Comments by the U.S. consul general in Kingston, Jamaica, in connection with a series of arrests for visa fraud hint at the size of the problem. Consular officers, he noted, "send a lot of people to the U.S.A. who have no right to go there," and there has grown up "a regular 'cottage industry' in the production of fraudulent Jamaican civil documents." He stated that almost every day of the week applicants presented altered or forged Jamaican passports, altered or forged Jamaican birth certificates, altered, forged or counterfeit U.S. birth certificates, and counterfeit Canadian Landed Immigrant Documents.[14] That the Jamaican situation is not unique is suggested by a firsthand account of visa issuance in the Philippines, where visa fraud also appears to be widespread.[15]

In addition, some fraud originates with individuals in this country who attempt to assist unqualified friends, relatives, or prospective employees to gain admission through sham marriages, false offers of employment, and other such actions. From whatever source, fraudulent applications or the anticipation of fraud impose an added burden on personnel involved in the screening process.

A critical question is whether the visa process in its present form can withstand the pressures arising from the rapidly growing demand for visas and from the widespread and increasingly sophisticated fraud. The answer would seem to be that considerably more personnel are needed to process visas, and new and improved procedures and facilities are needed to increase productivity if the system is to function satisfactorily.

14. *Jamaican Weekly Gleaner*, October 25, 1982.
15. Robert L. Lane, "Within the Visa Mill," *Foreign Service Journal*, vol. 17 (November 1981), pp. 26–30.

Figure 4-1. *Increases in Work Load and Positions, U.S. Bureau of Consular Affairs, Fiscal Years 1974–83*

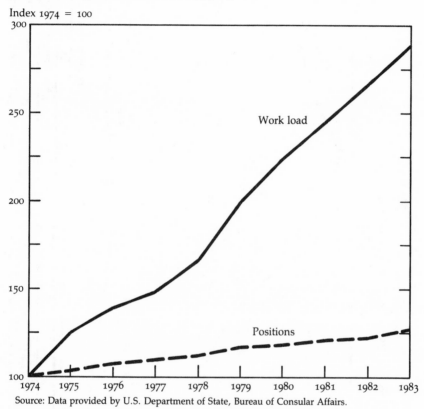

Index 1974 = 100

Source: Data provided by U.S. Department of State, Bureau of Consular Affairs.

Because visa work cannot be entirely separated from other consular activities, it is hard to tell exactly how many people are assigned to visa issuance or how the number has changed in recent years. The total number of consular positions abroad (as well as the numbers of foreign nationals assisting in consular work) has shown only modest increases since the early 1970s. According to the Bureau of Consular Affairs, personnel increased by about 22 percent between 1974 and 1982, whereas consular work increased by about 166 percent (figure 4-1), most of which was visa related (see figure 4-2).

Despite the tremendous increase in the work load, extensive

Figure 4-2. *Work Load, U.S. Bureau of Consular Affairs, by Type of Case, Fiscal Years 1972–85*

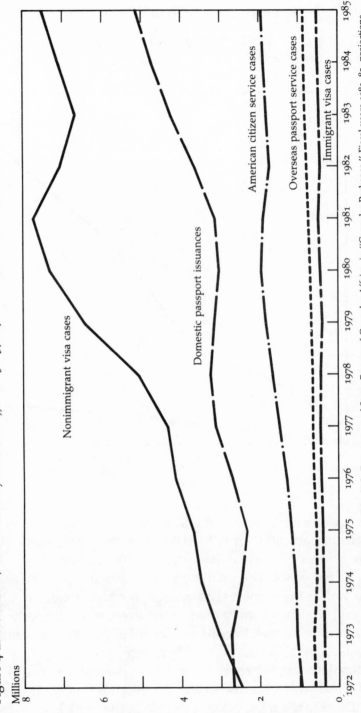

Source: Fiscal years 1972–82, data provided by U.S. Department of State, Bureau of Consular Affairs, in "Consular Packages." Fiscal years 1983–85, projections based on same data.

procedural changes in the processing of petitions for nonimmigrant visas have helped to improve productivity. The screening procedure has become more flexible, for one thing, and now relies on the perceptions of consular officers and Visa Office personnel to assess the degree of risk of visa abuse at particular posts. A Japanese or British national seeking a tourist visa, for example, is not likely to be required to appear before a consular officer for an interview. The visa can be granted by mail or through a travel agency. But in Jamaica, the Dominican Republic, or the Philippines, applicants are likely to be interviewed and all documents submitted in connection with the application scrutinized carefully. This different treatment reflects the judgment of the Visa Office and consular officials that the incidence of fraud and visa abuse is very low among Japanese and British nationals but that it is very high in the Caribbean countries and the Philippines.

Another procedural change has been an increase in the use of indefinite visas good for the life of the traveler's passport. Used on a large scale, this type of visa could substantially reduce the work load at some posts where traffic is high by sharply reducing the number of visa petitions.

During the last few years the Bureau of Consular Affairs has been trying to improve productivity by using computers to process visa applications. This effort began with the development of an automated nonimmigrant visa issuance system (ANVIS) that was installed at the U.S. Consulate in Toronto for experimental use.[16] ANVIS was designed to reduce the work load, speed up nonimmigrant visa processing, improve recordkeeping, and produce a secure, machine-readable nonimmigrant visa. Although the system has worked well in Toronto, it has not been placed elsewhere, mainly because the INS has not yet been able to develop a machine that could read the visas produced by ANVIS at ports of entry.

16. See Smith, *Nonimmigrant Visa Processing.*

The processing of applications for immigrant visas has undergone relatively little change. Each applicant must still be interviewed by consular officers before a visa is issued. However, the Bureau of Consular Affairs has developed and is deploying an Immigrant Visa Applicant Control System that will computerize the task to some extent. The purpose here, too, is to reduce the work load by using computers to process much of the information previously handled manually. As yet the system has been deployed in only five visa posts after having been tested in London in 1981.

Finally, to satisfy a legal requirement that a centralized name check be made of all visa applicants, the Bureau of Consular Affairs established a computerized data bank, which is now used to screen more than two-thirds of all visa applicants. Although these developments have helped consular posts cope with the increasing work load and are likely to be of even greater assistance in the future, the computer is clearly not the sole answer to the current problems. Visa issuance is a labor-intensive undertaking and much of the labor can only be done manually.

The most substantial gains in handling the rapidly increasing demand for entry to the United States are likely to come from a combination of expanded computer assistance, increased personnel, and a modification of visa requirements. One proposed modification that has been before the Congress since 1980 and that was included in the Simpson-Mazzoli bill is to waive the nonimmigrant visa requirement on a reciprocal basis for countries with very low visa refusal rates. Such a move would substantially reduce the work load in some consular posts and permit a shift of personnel to posts where the demand for visas is strong and the risk of visa abuse is high. The main point here, however, is that the procedures and technologies available today, if fully exploited, could improve the effectiveness of the visa issuance process as a means of controlling immigration.

Inspections

A visa does not guarantee that the bearer will be admitted to the United States; it merely authorizes travel to a U.S. port of entry where the alien will be inspected by an official of the INS. Only after the inspection has been completed will admission be granted or denied. In general, inspection at the port of entry involves no more than a quick examination of the visa and related travel documents to verify the bearer's eligibility for admission. Occasionally an inspecting official uncovers evidence of fraud or the intention to abuse a properly issued visa and denies admission.

Some analysts view this port-of-entry inspection as an unnecessary duplication of effort since it repeats what was done by a consular officer before the visa was issued.[17] For this reason in 1952 the Truman Immigration Commission urged that the practice be terminated.[18] Despite the duplication of effort and the possible inconvenience to a traveler who might be granted a visa but then be denied entry upon arrival, the procedure still appears to be a valuable tool in safeguarding against fraudulent entries. In the case of multiple entry and indefinite visas, port-of-entry inspection is the only feasible check on the traveler after the initial screening. Furthermore, the process would become indispensable if the proposed visa waiver policy was to be instituted. Some people also contend that the current procedure assures that the State and Justice departments will in fact share the responsibility for admitting aliens that has been designated to them.

Like visa issuance, the inspection process is severely strained by the great number of admissions. Here, too, inspections officials are under constant pressure to speed up the entry of

17. Charles Gordon, "The Need to Modernize Our Immigration Laws," *San Diego Law Review*, vol. 13 (1975), pp. 10–11.

18. *Whom We Shall Welcome: Report of the President's Commission on Immigration and Naturalization* (GPO, 1953), pp. 132–34.

travelers, but they find this difficult to do because inspection remains by and large a manual procedure and personnel increases have been far from adequate to compensate for the tremendous increase in the number of travelers.

Admitting Refugees

Like other aliens entering the country, refugees must be screened, issued appropriate documents, and admitted. But because their flight is usually sudden and because large numbers of people are generally involved—not to mention the fact that most of them do not meet the criteria established for routine immigrants such as the capacity to be self-supporting upon entry—refugees require more attention than other immigrants. Indeed, one of the immigration bureaucracy's most formidable challenges in recent years has been managing the admission of large numbers of refugees coming from several areas of the world under widely differing circumstances.

The procedures for admitting large numbers of refugees evolved over the past several years, but the sources of the refugees, the circumstances producing their flight, and the number of people involved have been so varied that it has been almost impossible for the United States to maintain a consistent and efficient procedure. Conditions were such that the postwar European refugees and the Cuban refugees who arrived during the 1960s could be admitted in a relatively organized manner, whereas other groups—such as the Hungarian refugees of 1956 and the many Indochinese who fled their countries immediately after the collapse of their governments or who took to sea in unseaworthy boats several months later—have had to be processed under much more difficult circumstances. More recently, the arrival without authorization of thousands of Haitians and Cubans claiming refugee status upon arrival has posed new and even more formidable procedural challenges to the immigration bureaucracy.

The screening and admission of large numbers of refugees

require the U.S. government to interact with international organizations and domestic voluntary organizations.[19] The broad objectives of the screening process are: to select for admission refugees who were employed by or have other special ties to the U.S. government, who have close relatives in the United States, or who have no practical alternatives to resettlement in this country; to exclude those whose presence might constitute a security risk; and to minimize the direct burden on the government for their support after their arrival.

Ordinarily, the screening process begins with a finding by the secretary of state that the people involved are indeed refugees and that they are of special interest to the United States for humanitarian or foreign policy reasons. Next, each refugee is registered, first with the United Nations High Commissioner for Refugees at their place of first asylum, and then with a recognized voluntary organization engaged in refugee resettlement, which gathers preliminary data essential in arranging resettlement.

Subsequently, all applications are reviewed by U.S. consular officials at or near the sites where the refugees are located and priority rankings are established, starting with those having close relatives residing in the United States, followed in order by former employees of the U.S. government, persons closely associated with the United States or with U.S. firms or organizations in their home country, and finally by other refugees with no other resettlement opportunities. This review is followed by a more detailed examination of each case by INS refugee specialists and it usually includes extensive interviews.

After the refugees' applications have been approved by INS officials, the cases are transferred to a voluntary agency, which tries to contact relatives or to find sponsors in the United States. Once a sponsor has been secured, the Intergovernmental Committee on Migration, a nongovernmental international

19. The principal actors in the handling of refugees are described in Charles B. Keely, *Global Refugee Policy: The Case for a Development-Oriented Strategy* (The Population Council, 1981), pp. 49–52.

refugee relief organization, arranges transportation to the United States. At the U.S. port of entry, the refugees are again examined by INS officials and then are finally admitted.

Because the procedure for screening refugees is itself time-consuming and relatively few INS officials are available to do the work, especially in emergencies, there are often long delays between a decision to admit a specified number of refugees and their arrival in this country. A point in its favor, however, is that this procedure gives the United States control of each refugee decision and allows for an orderly placement of refugees. These conditions do not exist when the United States becomes a place of first asylum, that is, when people in flight come directly to this country. In those circumstances the United States has little choice but to admit such refugees for resettlement. The sorry saga of the Haitian detainees underscores the problem here and the distastefulness of detention as a response.

Controlling the Flow across the Land Borders

Controlling the entry of aliens into the United States across its land borders is probably the immigration bureaucracy's most demanding responsibility in managing the immigrant flow. Although U.S. immigration laws prescribe essentially the same admission procedure for all aliens, the history, culture, and economic characteristics of the southern border region in particular have created special conditions that immigration policies have never been able to effectively handle. The task involves: (1) facilitating the entry of large numbers of aliens at designated entry points; (2) preventing unauthorized entries at places other than official entry points; and (3) responding informally and unofficially to the special needs of the border region for the movement of people.

Managing the routine flow of aliens across the land borders involves many of the same challenges and pressures associated with visa issuance and inspections. The flow here, for example, is also extremely heavy and the personnel insufficient. In 1981 alone, authorized entries across land borders by aliens exceeded 176 million, and that number has risen by more than 10 percent a year since then.[20] Although the United States has a strong interest in facilitating this traffic for the benefit of its economy and the relationship with its neighbors, the personnel and facilities needed to screen immigrants at the designated crossing points have been barely sufficient to do much more than a perfunctory screening.

Unauthorized entries are also a problem here, but in this case the special concern is the entries that take place away from designated crossing points. Such entries have been taking place since the mid-1800s and are a deeply entrenched practice, especially at the southern border. As noted earlier, evidence that unauthorized entries have been occurring on a large scale and are increasing rapidly and the continuing friction they create in U.S.-Mexico relations have made them the most prominent and controversial aspect of the flow control problem here.

Surreptitious overland entries are difficult to prevent in part because of the topographical features of the southern border region, which has few natural barriers along the more densely populated areas, and where, in addition, several cities straddle the border. Furthermore, economic forces on both sides have encouraged the clandestine movement of unemployed Mexican workers to this country. Although the United States has long relied on this pool of Mexican workers and has acted at times to attract it, current immigration laws allow few of these workers to enter legally. Illegal entry thus becomes their only alternative.

The Border Patrol—the unit within the INS that is responsible for preventing unauthorized entries and for apprehending those who enter the United States illegally in the border region—has never had the means to carry out this task effectively. Although the Border Patrol has apprehended over a million illegal entrants a year in at least three of the years since

20. Immigration statistics not cited by footnotes are from the Immigration and Naturalization Service, *1981 Statistical Yearbook.*

1977, another million or more probably succeed in entering illegally each year. Part of the problem is that the Border Patrol is small and has limited resources at its disposal to cope with the border management task. In fiscal year 1981 the daily on-duty force averaged about 2,690 officers on the immediate border, or a maximum of roughly 900 persons per shift (not allowing for leaves, illnesses, and the like) to patrol almost 2,000 miles of Mexican-U.S. border.[21] And in spite of the growing concern about illegal border crossings, the number of Border Patrol positions authorized for 1983 was only thirty-four more than the number for 1980.[22]

Another problem is that the smuggling rings that reportedly bring people into the United States surreptitiously for profit are apparently becoming more numerous and more sophisticated. According to several journalistic accounts and scattered data from the INS, smugglers transport people from all over the hemisphere across the U.S. land borders. Between 1972 and 1981, the number of smugglers apprehended by the INS nearly tripled, going from 4,564 to 12,643, while the number of smuggled aliens apprehended increased from 24,918 to 90,084 (their numbers exceeded 172,000 in 1979).

Although immigration law makes virtually no special concessions to allow movement across the U.S. land borders, some administrative procedures and informal discretionary actions have been used to facilitate relatively easy access to this country across the land borders. Canadian nationals are allowed entry without special entry documents, for example, while Mexicans can take advantage of two types of documents available for short-term entry. Form I-151 (the green card) is used by a small number of commuters (about 60,000) who cross the border daily to work in the United States. Ordinarily green cards are issued only to immigrants who intend to reside in the United States. However, the practice of issuing them to commuters has been upheld by federal courts, and, according to one INS

21. Data provided by the INS.
22. INS, *1980 Statistical Yearbook*, table 67.

general counsel, has been sanctioned by administrative interpretation and practice.[23] The majority of Mexicans use Form I-186 to enter the United States. This is a border-crossing card or special visitor's visa that permits the holder to stay in the United States up to seventy-two hours. It is obtainable from consular officials or INS officials at border-crossing points.

The inadequacies in flow management at the land borders can be viewed as two basic problems. One is the large and steadily rising number of travelers using official crossing points, which has made it difficult to ensure the smooth flow of eligible travelers to this country and prevent mala fide entries. This problem could be alleviated somewhat by developing travel documents that are relatively secure, valid for a long time, and machine readable. The other, more formidable problem, is that of clandestine entries, away from designated crossing points. Many observers think it is virtually impossible to prevent such entries. INS officials maintain, however, that if adequate resources, such as considerably more border personnel and equipment, were available, illegal entries could be drastically reduced.

Flow management problems are of great concern at home and abroad. Within the country, complaints about illegal immigration and about the effects of immigrants on many social programs have stimulated strong pressures to improve control of the flow. At the same time, the tourist and travel industries are eager to have procedures simplified, permitting easier access by foreign nationals. These objectives will not be easy to achieve in the face of the rapidly expanding volume of travelers.

Abroad, the screening process brings officials of the U.S. government into contact with foreign nationals in their own countries and at times arouses the concern of their governments about the treatment they receive. In this sense screening is a

23. Roger A. LaBracherie, "Aliens in the Fields: The 'Green-Card Commuter' Under the Immigration and Naturalization Laws," *Stanford Law Review*, vol. 21 (1969), pp. 1750–76.

quasi-diplomatic activity, and thus much U.S. goodwill abroad may hinge on the efficiency of the operation. The long lines and extremely uncomfortable or inadequate waiting facilities typical of some consular posts almost certainly contribute to ill will toward the United States. An adequately staffed, equipped, and directed flow management effort, particularly with respect to the southern border, is obviously less likely to trigger conflict with other countries or ill will toward the United States than an inadequate and ineffective one.

Internal Supervision and Control

Once aliens arrive in the United States the INS has the responsibility to ensure that they comply with the conditions of their entry and depart upon the expiration of their authorized stay. Although most nonimmigrants or temporary visitors voluntarily comply with the law, many do not. Some enter the country legally with the intention of violating the conditions of their visas, others decide to do so after entry, and still others slip in surreptitiously across the land borders. The INS is responsible for the apprehension and expulsion of all those who fail to comply with the terms of their admission or who enter surreptitiously. These tasks—which, for the sake of convenience, can be called the "control" functions of the INS— are the means by which the country maintains the integrity of its immigration laws. However, they are now performed so poorly as to represent the most glaring failure of the immigration bureaucracy.

The poor performance is not difficult to explain. One problem is that the INS has simply failed to develop adequate facilities and procedures to carry out its control responsibilities effectively. Another is that many of the procedures employed by the INS are outdated and of dubious legality. Although many of these procedures have been challenged in recent years, the INS has not seriously evaluated and modified them. Still another problem is the public's continuing ambivalence about and distaste for closely monitoring, apprehending, and expelling aliens who violate immigration laws.

Lack of Enforcement Capabilities

The INS is not unique among government agencies in having more to do than the resources with which to do it. What is striking about this agency, however, is the extent of the discrepancy between its resources and its responsibilities. That the INS lacks the capability to enforce U.S. immigration laws is evident in virtually every area of its performance, particularly in its handling of data. Journalistic accounts of INS data-handling problems are sometimes accompanied by pictures of stacks of aging cardboard boxes, bulging and faded manila folders and envelopes, and rooms full of documents in disarray—this in an era of incredible achievement in data storage and data-handling technology.

The agency obviously cannot perform its mission effectively under these circumstances. It must be able to handle a multitude of data. At a minimum the INS should be able to gather and analyze data for internal management purposes and for fulfilling routine services, including current information on the number of aliens admitted to the country, the number who depart, and those who fail to depart at the required time. Because it has not been able to do this, demands for such information by the government have at times created major crises for the agency.

The INS has two basic systems for obtaining this kind of information. One is the nonimmigrant document control system (NIDC), which is supposed to collect: (1) routine information on each alien admitted and the alien's address in the United States (derived from the arrival segment of Form I-94, which is submitted to INS inspectors by the alien upon admission); (2) change-of-status data for nonresident aliens who change their status (from one visa category to another) while in the

United States; and (3) data on departures (derived from the appropriate segment of Form I-94 submitted to the carrier by the alien upon departure). The NIDC system should allow the INS to determine at any time the number of nonimmigrant aliens in the country and their status. However, this is not possible at the present time because the INS has not been able to keep the data in the NIDC system current. Nor has it been able to ensure that the data are reliable. In September 1981 the INS conceded that it had a backlog of about 30 million I-94 forms and more than 600,000 extensions of temporary stay to be processed.[24] In addition, the number of keypunch errors in the processed data was extremely high and the system contained only a portion of the required data on departures.[25]

The second data system, which was abandoned by Congress in 1981 to save money, was based on information from alien registration cards that all aliens were required to fill out with their address and certain other basic information and submit to the INS in January of each year. Although the INS administered the annual reporting system, the agency did not know the level of compliance and made minimal use of the data. The individual files on the cases handled by the INS should be another major source of data, but the agency's antiquated manual storage system and the fact that some of its files are held in its field offices make them of limited value.

The inability of the INS to supervise or maintain data on nonresident aliens was vividly demonstrated by the agency's efforts in November 1979 to determine the number and whereabouts of Iranian students in the country and to expel those who had violated the terms of their admission. Since foreign students constitute a relatively small segment of the nonresident alien population, they should not be very difficult to track down. However, the INS was unable to determine how many Iranian students were in the country or where they were studying. In an effort to comply with the attorney general's

24. "Backlog Grows on Alien Files," *New York Times*, November 22, 1981.
25. GAO, *Prospects Dim for Effectively Enforcing Immigration Laws*, pp. 20–21.

directive that their status be reviewed so that violators could be expelled, the INS shifted about 1,200 employees from their usual tasks to that of verifying the status of an estimated 73,600 Iranian students. Almost a year and $3.3 million later, the agency still was unable to determine the exact size of this student population or the whereabouts of many of its members.[26]

Educational institutions authorized by the INS to admit foreign students might have been an alternative source of information, but the INS has failed to remain informed about the status and activities of these institutions. A GAO report found, for example, that of 1,009 schools in the Los Angeles area authorized to admit foreign students, the INS was unable to contact 300, and of 500 in the Washington, D.C., area it was unable to contact 200.[27] Lack of supervision or contact with approved schools has also created opportunities for abuses. Since educational institutions have a direct financial interest in admitting foreign students, many have been aggressively recruiting students abroad, and some are alleged to have allowed the I-20 forms, the document required for entry as a foreign student, to be sold abroad to individuals seeking to migrate to this country.

Understandably, the problems in remaining informed about the much larger population of other nonresident aliens are considerably greater since the government in this country does not routinely monitor the movement of individuals. There is a large and growing gap between the reported number of aliens who enter the country and the number of departures documented annually. In 1979 the INS conducted an experiment to determine the status of aliens whose departure had not been verified by selecting at random from the NIDC system the names of 3,734 aliens who had apparently overstayed. The

26. General Accounting Office, *Controls over Nonimmigrant Aliens Remain Ineffective* (GAO, 1980), pp. 4–6. Also see Bernard Weinraub, "U.S. Immigration Bureaucracy," *New York Times*, January 17, 1980.

27. GAO, *Controls over Nonimmigrant Aliens Remain Ineffective*, p. 5.

study established that one-third of the sample had indeed left the country, but the other two-thirds could not be accounted for.[28]

Experiences like these illustrate the inadequacy of the most basic element in the administration of immigration policy—the INS data-gathering system. Undoubtedly the INS problem is partly a result of the rapidly rising number of aliens entering the country, but it also reflects the long-standing inattention to these needs by both the executive branch and Congress. Other units within the government that must maintain current information on large numbers of individuals, such as the Social Security Administration and the Federal Bureau of Investigation, have been able to maintain reasonably effective and reliable data systems.

The lack of institutional capacity at the INS is equally evident in the way the agency investigates fraud and misrepresentation by aliens, ascertains violations by aliens of the terms of their admission, and apprehends and expels those found to be in the country illegally. These are difficult and laborious tasks. They are performed primarily by the Investigations and the Detention and Deportation divisions of the INS, both of which have unrealistically small staffs and support facilities. In 1980, just over 1,000 INS officials, about a tenth of total INS personnel, were responsible for apprehending illegal immigrants and for investigating a wide range of suspected immigration law violations nationwide. Since then that number may have declined along with the overall decline in the agency's total authorized strength. The Detention and Deportation Division, equally understaffed, has a total of about 1,100 individuals for all detention-related activities. Moreover, the INS has had a chronic shortage of detention facilities, sometimes so severe as to force curtailment of some investigative activities because the agency was unable to house the aliens being apprehended.

28. GAO, *Prospects Dim for Effectively Enforcing Immigration Law*, pp. 20–21.

Outdated Enforcement Procedures

The INS has been severely handicapped in carrying out its investigative activities by some ineffective and highly controversial procedures. There is really no entirely effective and pleasant way to identify, apprehend, and expel illegal aliens. Not only do these activities frequently evoke public criticism, some have been challenged in federal courts as violations of civil rights, with the result that the INS has been forced to modify some of its procedures. Even where the procedures have withstood these challenges, lengthy litigation has been disruptive and costly for the INS.

INS investigative procedures have included random searches of vehicles in the vicinity of the land borders thought likely to contain illegal immigrants and interrogation of the occupants about their immigration status; random questioning of individuals in the interior of the country who appear or sound foreign-born to determine their status; "sweeps" through neighborhoods or gathering places believed to be occupied by illegal aliens; and raids on workplaces where they are believed to be employed. (The last two methods are called "area control operations.") These practices are based on very broad legislative authorizations to INS investigators, such as section 287a(1) and (3) of the amended Immigration and Nationality Act, which states:

> Any officer or employee of the service authorized under regulations prescribed by the Attorney General shall have the power without warrant to interrogate *any alien or person believed to be an alien* as to his right to be or to remain in the United States; and within a reasonable distance from any external boundary of the United States, to *board and search* for aliens any vessel within the territorial waters of the United States and any railway or aircraft, conveyance, or vehicle. (Emphasis added.)

The attorney general, incidentally, has interpreted "reasonable distance" to mean within 100 air miles of the border.

Starting in about 1968, the courts began to subject INS activities to increasing scrutiny under the Fourth Amendment's protection of individuals against arbitrary searches and seizures. For one thing, they required INS investigators to show reasonable cause for searches and seizures. In addition, they attempted to distinguish between rules governing searches and seizures at the country's borders or their functional equivalent and such actions away from the borders. These court actions demonstrate the difficulty of balancing the national interest in the effective control of immigration against the protection of individual rights. The results of their decisions thus far have complicated the control effort, increased somewhat the protection of individuals from arbitrary INS actions, and demonstrated the need for drastically different strategies by the INS.

In 1968 the Supreme Court ruled that when an individual is restrained through physical force or show of authority, a "seizure" has occurred, and the individual must be granted Fourth Amendment protection.[29] The reasonableness of a seizure, the Court suggested, depends on a balance between the public interest and the individual's right to be free of arbitrary interference by law enforcement officers. If a seizure was to be justified, the Court said, the law enforcement agent had to be able to point to specific and articulable facts, which, taken together with rational inferences from those facts, reasonably warrant that intrusion.

The Court subsequently invalidated some INS control methods that it found to impinge unreasonably on the individual's right to protection from unreasonable searches and seizures. In 1973, for example, it ruled that the search of vehicles by roving INS investigators without a warrant away from the border was a violation of the Fourth Amendment.[30] However, in 1975 the Court upheld brief vehicular stops by roving patrols based on "reasonable suspicion." In such cases, it ruled, "The officer may question the driver and passengers about citizenship

29. *Terry* v. *Ohio*, 392 U.S. 1 (1968).
30. *Almeida-Sanchez* v. *U.S.*, 413 U.S. 266 (1973).

and immigration status, and he may ask them to explain suspicious circumstances, but any further detention or search must be based on consent or probable cause. . . . We are unwilling," the Court declared, "to dispense entirely with the requirement that officers must have a reasonable suspicion to justify roving patrol stops."[31]

The requirement of the courts that INS investigators show probable cause in undertaking searches and seizures as part of their enforcement responsibility has led to some changes in long-standing INS investigative practices. These changes, although not drastic, undoubtedly have increased the difficulty of conducting investigations. Even though the court requires investigators to have reasonable cause for stopping a vehicle and interrogating its occupants, the court has been neither rigid nor definitive about this requirement. On the contrary, it has recognized the difficulty of conducting an essential law enforcement task under especially challenging circumstances and has exhibited substantial flexibility in the kind of factors it considers acceptable as a showing of probable cause. Moreover, it has continued to allow brief checks of all vehicles by the INS at fixed, reasonably located checkpoints without a showing of probable cause.

The Court's flexibility in handling the probable cause requirement is further reflected in one of the most recent of the search and seizure decisions, in which it held that INS investigators acted within the Constitution when a roving patrol stopped a vehicle carrying deportable aliens in the Arizona desert. The Court asserted that "in determining what cause is sufficient to authorize police to stop a vehicle, the totality of the circumstances—the whole picture must be taken into account."[32] From that picture, the Court suggested, a trained officer may draw inferences and make deductions. The effect of these decisions, however, has been to make INS investigators

31. *U.S.* v. *Brignoni-Ponce*, 422 U.S. 873 (1975).
32. *U.S.* v. *Cortez*, 101 S.Ct. 690 (1981).

more sensitive to Fourth Amendment issues in planning their investigative activities.

The legal situation is more murky with respect to INS investigative activities in the interior of the country, particularly its area control operations. Court decisions have required INS compliance with Fourth Amendment standards that have more far-reaching effects on INS investigative practices than the border cases. Two issues are especially noteworthy. One is the INS practice of interrogating individuals in the interior of the country who are suspected of being in the country illegally. The other involves unannounced inspections or raids of workplaces where such aliens are believed to be employed.

The first issue was considered in a 1975 case in which a federal district court ruled that any detention of an individual for questioning must be based on "reasonable suspicion" of unlawful presence. The court decided that a detention did not occur, however, if the individual being questioned was free to walk away from the investigator.[33] In 1977 a New York district court discarded the view that an individual is not detained if free to leave and suggested that any questioning at all is intrusive and detentive.[34] The effect of this decision is that the once widely used practice of randomly interrogating individuals on a street corner or other public place can no longer be routinely used by the INS. Another court had also enjoined the INS from approaching people in their homes, businesses, or workplaces without reasonable suspicion that their presence in the United States is illegal.[35] Such evidence, the court further ruled, cannot be only language or nationality.

The trend toward the imposition of stricter constitutional standards on INS investigators by the courts also has affected one of the most widely known and controversial INS investigative procedures—raiding a workplace where deportable aliens are believed to be employed. For years, INS investigators

33. *Illinois Migrant Council v. Pilliod,* 398 F. Supp. 882 (N.D. Ill. 1975).
34. *Marquez v. Kiley,* 436 F. Supp. 882 (S.D.N.Y. 1977).
35. *Illinois Migrant Council v. Pilliod.*

conducted these raids or area control activities on the basis of tips, hunches, or rumors, and without warrants of any kind. Gradually, the courts have come to insist that INS investigators obtain warrants for these raids.

The degree of specificity required in these warrants became an issue in a case resulting from a raid by INS investigators on a Washington, D.C., restaurant in November 1978. The INS raid was conducted pursuant to a warrant issued by a federal judge on the basis of a showing by the INS of probable cause that deportable aliens were on the premises. In a suit by the restaurant seeking injunctive, declaratory, and compensatory relief, the U.S. District Court for the District of Columbia found the warrant invalid because it failed to name each alien sought and was thus a violation of the Fourth Amendment rights of the aliens. The U.S. Court of Appeals reversed this decision, finding the warrant as descriptive as was reasonably possible and reflecting a reasonable balance between the individual's right to privacy and the public interest in effective enforcement of immigration laws.[36] Thus, while continuing to hold the INS to the basic Fourth Amendment principle in its investigative activities, the court exhibited a willingness to consider the special enforcement problems that the INS faces.

Expelling aliens who have been apprehended has also become an increasingly difficult undertaking for the INS since these actions have been subjected to increased judicial scrutiny and public opposition in recent years. Ordinarily, the INS takes one of three courses upon apprehending aliens found to be deportable. If the individuals have family or other ties in this country that provide a legal basis for acquiring immigrant status, they may be allowed to adjust their status while remaining in the country under an indefinite order from the INS to depart. (In other words, the INS orders the aliens to

---

36. *Blackie's House of Beef, Inc.* v. *Castillo*, 480 F. Supp. 1078 (D.D.C. 1979); 659 F.2d 1211 (D.C. Cir. 1981). For a discussion of the issues in the case, see Stephen J. Anaya, "Constitutional Law: Protection against Illegal Search and Seizure," *Harvard International Law Journal*, vol. 22 (Fall 1981), pp. 670–76.

leave, but then says the aliens can remain and have their status legalized.) Other apprehended aliens are permitted to depart voluntarily and, depending on the circumstances, to do so with or without INS supervision. Finally, others who either refuse to leave voluntarily, are believed likely to abscond if released, or have been repeated violators are deported. Only a very small fraction of those apprehended each year are deported. The rest depart voluntarily, adjust their status, or abscond.

Voluntary departure is often advantageous to both the INS and the apprehended aliens. Deportation proceedings generally take a long time, often require detention of the alien at public expense, and require legal counsel to represent the INS. Deportation proceedings can also be unpleasant and costly for the alien, and if deportation occurs, the alien is prohibited from reentering the country. Voluntary departure eliminates these costs to both the INS and the alien. Some people argue, however, that the INS abuses the option of voluntary departure by forcing aliens to opt for it when they may have a legal basis for staying and that it often fails to notify the aliens of their right to obtain legal assistance in contesting their expulsion.[37] Moreover, an increasing number of aliens refuse to depart voluntarily, thereby extending their stay for the several months or even years that may be required to complete deportation proceedings. For others, fighting expulsion is simply one more means of further burdening and perhaps undermining an already seriously overburdened INS.

Confronted with court decisions outlawing or restricting some of its basic investigative procedures, the INS often has attempted to conform by discontinuing the offending practices. More significantly, these legal developments, as well as the high cost and labor-intensive nature of the investigative activities in the interior of the country, have prompted the INS to reduce its emphasis on apprehending and expelling deportable

37. U.S. Commission on Civil Rights, *The Tarnished Golden Door: Civil Rights Issues in Immigration* (GPO, 1980), pp. 109–10.

aliens already in the country and to stress instead increased efforts to prevent illegal entries. They have also prompted INS officials to try to focus more on combating organized illegal schemes like smuggling, sham marriages, and the production of fraudulent documents than on apprehending individual deportable aliens within the country.

These are rational decisions, given the demands on the INS and the resources at its disposal, but they signify a partial abandonment of a vital part of the enforcement responsibility. Moreover, the diminishing effectiveness of the internal control efforts of the INS—especially the declining likelihood that a deportable alien in the country will be apprehended and expelled—makes the immigrant flow more difficult to manage because illegal residence comes to be perceived as almost risk free and therefore a good investment by those abroad who seek employment here.

Public Attitudes toward Internal Control

Although the public is overwhelmingly opposed to illegal immigration and would like to see it ended or at least sharply curtailed (see table 2-2), many who are concerned with immigration matters tend to ignore the enforcement problems that the INS is facing or appear to be ambivalent about current enforcement policies. There are no reliable measures of public opinion on this subject, and thus there are no firm indications of exactly how the public feels about apprehending and expelling aliens. However, public reaction to specific, widely publicized cases of apprehension or expulsion by the INS reveals sharply divergent views. For example, in April 1982 when the INS undertook a brief nationwide effort to apprehend and expel deportable aliens in well-paying jobs, the effort was greeted by widespread protests, especially from activists and the leaders of national and local organizations. The Roman Catholic archbishop and the Episcopal bishop in Denver, Colorado, reportedly signed statements protesting the actions.

Other church officials offered to provide food and shelter to deportable aliens who sought to hide from the INS,[38] while Senator Alan Cranston, Democrat of California, complained that the raids "are sowing dangerous seeds of racial and ethnic conflict in California"; and Tony Bonilla, executive director of the League of United Latin American Citizens (LULAC), called the effort "a grandstand play by the INS to cover up the inadequacies of the Reagan economic policies."[39]

Procedural indiscretions by INS investigators sometimes trigger public opposition to INS investigations, but this reaction often masks a complex array of public attitudes toward immigration, individual rights, and the responsibilities of government, and of course toward the special interests some people have at stake. Many people, for example, seem to view INS efforts to apprehend and expel illegal aliens as part of a struggle (between the all-powerful state and the individual at his most vulnerable) in which they cannot perceive the alien as a villain, even though they might be opposed to illegal immigration in general.

Many others, such as some employers, merchants, real estate investors, and even many local public officials, tend to think that the aliens provide more benefits than disadvantages and are unsympathetic with efforts to expel them. Meanwhile, many religious and humanitarian organizations focus on the human predicament involved in illegal immigration, believing that their mission is to assist the immigrants involved. Finally, some ethnic groups see today's illegal aliens as products of the same forces that brought them or their ancestors to this country and are reluctant to deny them the opportunities they experienced. These public attitudes almost certainly have a chilling effect on the INS and deprive investigators of the cooperation of the public that would make the task easier. They might also

---

38. "Roundup of Aliens Meeting Problems," *New York Times*, May 30, 1982; and "Nearly 1,000 Are Seized in a Job Sweep of Aliens," *New York Times*, April 27, 1982.
39. "250 Illegal Aliens Seized in 2d Sweep," *Chicago Tribune*, April 28, 1982.

account for some of Congress's inattentiveness to the needs of the immigration bureaucracy.

Meeting Service Responsibilities

In addition to performing its management and control functions, the immigration bureaucracy is expected to disseminate information on the immigration process to the public, provide immigration-related administrative or adjudicatory services, and manage the process of naturalization. Much of the recent criticism of the immigration bureaucracy centers on the serious delays or other shortcomings in the performance of these routine services.[40]

Information Services

Although most of the immigration bureaucracy's services are rendered to aliens already in the country, the demand for these services is global. Often the first contact a prospective traveler has with the United States comes about as the result of a request for information from a U.S. consular officer in the traveler's home country. Adequate and timely information helps the individual determine how to apply for a visa and whether he or she is likely to qualify for admission to the United States. Screening is thus made more efficient and less traumatic for the individuals involved.

Within the United States, information needs are many and varied. Citizens and aliens alike may want to know how to help a relative enter the country, how to bring a foreign worker into the country, and how an alien already here obtains an extension of a temporary stay or an adjustment of status. Public officials and analysts, meanwhile, may need information about levels, trends, and problems in immigration. A prompt response to these requests for information is beneficial not only

40. Commission on Civil Rights, *Tarnished Golden Door*, pp. 31–43.

to those who seek the information but also to the immigration bureaucracy, since it helps the public use the information services intelligently. Moreover, many of the individuals and organizations that seek information from the immigration bureaucracy in turn assist others with their immigration problems. Indeed, the several private voluntary organizations that help individuals deal with immigration problems play a vital role by reducing the demands on the immigration bureaucracy.

Requests for information from within the United States are handled primarily by the INS. Although there is no way to measure the demand precisely, the range of information requested and the many sources from which the demands come point to a considerable load for the INS, one which it has not been handling well. Testifying before a subcommittee of the House Appropriations Committee, Representative Eilberg complained:

> The public is required to wait a minimum of two hours in line at the major offices to obtain an answer to a simple question. To reach an INS office by telephone requires persistency and an enormous amount of patience, and then once through, one is never sure if the relevant reply will be forthcoming, or for that matter accurate.[41]

INS Commissioner Leonel Castillo painted a similar picture in testimony before the House Subcommittee on Appropriations in 1978, reporting that upon taking office at the Los Angeles district office, he observed that lines of people seeking service the next day began to form at midnight, telephone calls went unanswered, and it took a long wait in line simply to obtain routine forms.[42] There have been substantial improvements at Los Angeles and some other district offices since these comments were made, but similar conditions continue in other areas (for example, Miami). The long lines, crowded conditions, and unanswered telephones in turn reflect severe deficiencies

---

41. *Departments of State, Justice, and Commerce . . . Appropriations, 1978*, Hearings, pt. 7, p. 446.
42. Quoted in Commission on Civil Rights, *Tarnished Golden Door*, p. 31.

in the organization and management of district offices, especially with respect to the handling of case records.[43]

Adjudicative Services

The INS also adjudicates or otherwise responds administratively to petitions such as requests for an extension of stay by nonresident aliens, requests for adjustment of status from nonimmigrant or provisional entrants (refugees) to immigrant status, or requests for a review of an adverse decision affecting an alien's continued stay in the country. That the INS has been unable to respond adequately to these service demands is reflected in the massive backlogs and long delays that have persisted in its adjudicatory work.

In conceding that routine requests for adjudicatory actions take an inordinately long time, INS Commissioner Castillo explained in testimony to the U.S. Civil Rights Commission that the resources needed to do the job were far from adequate to meet the sharp increase in the requests for these actions.[44] Under his leadership the INS undertook a crash program to clear up the backlog of cases and ensure a quick response to such requests. That effort reduced the backlog only temporarily, however, and was insufficient to improve the situation over the long term. Futhermore, it compelled the agency to reduce its activities in other areas and so merely shifted the inadequate performance to other locations. According to a study by the House Committee on Government Operations, the situation had not improved much by 1980. There were still massive backlogs and no systematic procedure for adjudications.[45]

Since that report, the INS has acted to improve its adjudicative service. It has established two "remote processing centers" where applications not requiring interviews with the

43. *Immigration and Naturalization Service Records Management Problems*, H. Rept. 96-1459, House Committee on Government Operations, 96 Cong. 2 sess. (GPO, 1980), pp. 10–11.

44. Commission on Civil Rights, *Tarnished Golden Door*, p. 35.

45. *INS Records Management Problems*, H. Rept. 96-1459, pp. 32–34.

applicants can be processed speedily without the distractions of other activities in the district offices. It has also begun to grant a standard six-month stay to visitors (B-2 visa holders), thereby reducing the number of requests for extension of stay.

Naturalization Services

After five years of continuous residence in the United States, an immigrant is entitled to apply for citizenship by naturalization. Up to 1906 the process of naturalization was administered by the states, but inconsistencies and abuses were common. When the Bureau of Immigration and Naturalization was created in June of that year, the federal government assumed the responsibility.

Naturalization proceedings are conducted by federal district courts or by qualified state courts upon the recommendation of the INS. Before making that recommendation, the INS must ensure that each applicant for naturalization is qualified under the existing laws specifying the conditions for naturalization. With few exceptions, a recommendation by the INS to grant or deny naturalization is accepted by the courts. The naturalization process is therefore primarily administrative, and the courts merely perform the final legal and symbolic rites.

Less than a third of the eligible lawful immigrants seek naturalization, but as overall immigration increases so does the demand for naturalization. For example, during the 1970s the number of persons naturalized annually increased by more than 46 percent, from 108,000 in 1971 to 157,938 in 1980 after reaching a high of 173,535 in 1978.[46] Here, too, the INS has been extremely slow (in 1981 the average waiting time for naturalization after the initial filing with the INS was about fourteen months), again because limited resources are allocated to such service activities.

Throughout the history of the immigration bureaucracy, service responsibilities have received much less emphasis than enforcement responsibilities. To some extent, this situation is

---

46. INS, *1980 Statistical Yearbook*, table 23.

understandable. Aliens, the principal constituency being served, are generally patient, politically powerless, and unwilling or reluctant to complain. Given the perennial scarcity of resources to support government activities, the INS has concentrated whatever resources are available on its urgent enforcement responsibilities. Toward the end of the 1970s the INS changed its focus somewhat in an effort to cope with the rapidly growing service demands and in order to improve the agency's image.

Refugee Resettlement

Unlike immigrants who deliberately decide to relocate, refugees usually are forced to flee their homelands without preparation and often without money or the skills necessary to become immediately self-supporting in this country. They have therefore needed special assistance. At first a number of private voluntary organizations assumed responsibility for refugee resettlement, but the federal government gradually became involved, first by providing small amounts of money to defray the initial cost of relocation and resettlement.[47] Later, with the beginning of a large-scale flow of refugees from Cuba, the Congress created a Cuban Refugee Program to fund their resettlement in 1964. It responded similarly to the Indochinese refugees in 1975 by creating an Indochinese Refugee Assistance Program. It also provided small sums of money on a one-for-one matching basis to voluntary organizations for the initial expenses associated with the resettlement of Soviet Jews and other refugees. These programs were then replaced by the Refugee Act of 1980, which for the first time established a comprehensive refugee resettlement program funded almost entirely by the federal government.

As a single program under the jurisdiction of a newly created Office of Refugee Resettlement, the new program has brought increased federal funds and a new order to refugee resettlement.

47. *Review of U.S. Refugee Resettlement Programs and Policies*, prepared for the Senate Committee on the Judiciary, 96 Cong. 2 sess. (GPO, 1980), pp. 19–26.

It has also placed direct responsibility for actual resettlement activities on state governments and has gone a long way toward standardizing approaches to resettlement by requiring that, as a condition for receiving federal reimbursement of expenses for refugee assistance, each state submit a state plan for managing refugee assistance that meets certain criteria. Specifically, the states are required to designate an agency for developing and administering the plan, describe how cash and other assistance will be used to promote economic self-sufficiency among refugees, identify a state official responsible for coordinating public and private resources for refugee resettlement, and prepare detailed plans for caring for unaccompanied refugee children and for identifying and treating refugees needing medical care. Although this new approach to refugee resettlement makes the states the principal agent in refugee resettlement, localities—cities or counties—provide most of the actual services directly or under contracts to voluntary organizations, which continue to provide many of the services necessary to facilitate speedy resettlement.

The goal of the resettlement effort is to make the refugee self-sufficient as quickly as possible after entry. Toward this end, attempts are made to provide each refugee family with the basic necessities for a comfortable existence by this society's standards, with language and other training essential to obtain employment, and with financial assistance until economic self-sufficiency is achieved. Federal monetary assistance now lasts for eighteen months, by which time it is assumed that refugees will have achieved self-sufficiency. (Refugee children are provided financial assistance indefinitely.) Most refugees are able to find jobs and become self-sufficient within the specified period, but many remain dependent long after that time and become beneficiaries of whatever public assistance programs they qualify for. Because many of these programs are partly funded by states and localities, large numbers of dependent refugees can become a major financial burden on states and localities once federal support is discontinued.

Several other problems have come in the way of the refugee resettlement effort, some of which became apparent with the unauthorized influx of Mariel Bay Cubans and the Haitian boat people. The current laws and administrative procedures proved inadequate for processing aliens coming directly to this country without prior approval and claiming to be refugees. Not only did they severely tax the resources of the south Florida jurisdictions in which they arrived, but the circumstances of their arrival meant that they did not fit into the scheme established in the 1980 law and thus makeshift arrangements had to be made for processing them, detaining those deemed inadmissible, and funding the resettlement of those who were not detained.

Another problem has been the continuing cost of assisting those refugees who do not quickly become self-sufficient, as the law anticipates. As federal refugee assistance funds run out, much of that responsibility falls on state and local governments, who have become increasingly concerned about the growing burden such assistance imposes on them. Still another problem is that in some localities resettlement assistance has generated concern and hostility among some segments of the low-income population who believe that refugees are drawing away resources and opportunities that they have been seeking without success. This dissatisfaction has remained an undercurrent in some localities, while in others it has erupted into major controversies and even violence in a few cases. These problems have imposed strains on the immigration bureaucracy, on several other federal government agencies, and on localities. However, the country's overall handling of refugee resettlement is one of the most improved areas of immigration policy enforcement.

The Character of the Enforcement Problem

One of the few points about which almost everyone knowledgeable about immigration seems to agree is that the administration of immigration policy is inadequate and that the situation is growing worse. When it comes to identifying the problems and deciding what should be done about them, however, there is no such consensus. Not only do the problems vary from one segment of the immigration bureaucracy to another, they are perceived differently in different segments of the federal government.

The INS, the Office of Management and Budget (OMB), and Congress tend to emphasize different causes of these problems. INS officials have long thought that insufficient funds and the resulting lack of personnel are the primary causes, and that more money would help considerably to turn things around. The OMB, which controls INS budget requests to Congress and ostensibly reflects the administration's thinking, has tended to stress instead that flaws in enforcement strategies and priorities are the principal causes, and thus it has consistently slashed INS requests for increased funds, arguing that administrative and policy changes were required before any significant infusion of new funds. After drastically reducing Justice Department budget recommendations to increase the INS budget and personnel in fiscal year 1980, an OMB budget examiner said as much to a study team of the House Government Operations Committee: some of the INS's problems in handling resources result from a long-standing conflict between enforcement and service responsibilities. He complained that the agency put too much emphasis on enforcement and too little on service and pledged that "in the future, OMB is going to place more attention onto the service aspects of INS and place the INS enforcement responsibilities in a holding pattern."[48]

The OMB's assessment and its plan to place support for enforcement on hold are remarkable in view of the overwhelming evidence of across-the-board administrative failures. What is even more remarkable is that after urging the INS to request

---

48. *INS Records Management Problems*, H. Rept. 96-1459, pp. 80–81.

supplemental appropriations for improving service activities, the OMB turned down the request.

Congress has also been reluctant to approve large new allocations for the INS, mainly because of what it perceives to be major administrative problems at the INS. Several hearings by a number of committees have focused on a wide range of such problems. Indeed, after appropriating $3.7 million in fiscal year 1980 to automate the INS district offices, Congress halted the effort because INS officials had failed to plan the undertaking properly. The Senate Appropriations Committee cut the fiscal year 1981 appropriation by $2 million, noting that "although the Committee is vigorously supportive of the automation of the INS, it would be irresponsible to appropriate more funds in the absence of an approved plan."[49] The committee also noted that it was difficult to appropriate increased funds for the INS to enforce immigration policy in the absence of a clear, discernible policy, and in effect decided to hold the line on new funding until the administration's enforcement policy was clarified. In so doing, it joined several other congressional committees in urging the development of plausible immigration policies and enforcement procedures and improved management by the INS before committing substantial new resources to the enforcement effort.

Congress gave considerable attention to the needs of the immigration bureaucracy in its consideration of the Simpson-Mazzoli bill. Both houses voted to suspend the visitor's visa requirement on a reciprocal basis for some countries, and the House authorized substantially increased funding for enforcement, stressing the addition of personnel and equipment to prevent illegal immigration.

These differing views about the reasons for the poor performance of the INS, along with the lack of public support for increased funding of administrative activities, help to explain

---

49. *Departments of State, Justice, and Commerce, the Judiciary, and Related Agencies Appropriation Bill, 1981*, S. Rept. 96-949, 96 Cong. 2 sess. (GPO, 1980), p. 26.

Table 4-2. *Immigration and Naturalization Service Budget Requests, Appropriations, and Rates of Change, Fiscal Years 1969–84*
Figures in millions of dollars

Fiscal year	INS request	Congressional appropriation[a]	Percentage change over previous year's appropriation[b]
1969	87.8	87.3	. . .
1970	94.9	94.6	2.5
1971	112.9	112.4	14.5
1972	130.6	130.6	12.9
1973	135.1	135.1	−2.8
1974	143.3	143.3	−4.9
1975	184.1	175.9	13.6
1976	209.7	208.0	12.5
1977	221.6	234.0	6.0
1978	256.3	266.5	6.2
1979	298.0	309.3	4.8
1980	304.4	318.5	−10.5
1981	347.7	351.0	−0.2
1982	363.4	446.5	21.1
1983	524.6	488.9	6.3
1984	512.6	501.3	n.a.

Source: *Congressional Quarterly Almanac,* annual volumes, 1968–83.
n.a. Not available.
a. Total fiscal year appropriation (includes supplemental appropriation).
b. Adjusted for inflation, based on the consumer price index in U.S. Bureau of the Census, *Statistical Abstract of the United States: 1984* (Government Printing Office, 1983), p. 485.

why there have been only modest increases in the INS budget for most of the past decade, even though its problems are widely acknowledged. The growth of the budget, from $87.3 million in 1969 to $501.3 million in 1984 (see table 4-2), is due in large part to inflation and the overall increase in government spending during this period. The real budget increases have been modest increments that have allowed the INS to improve only slightly the routine conduct of enforcement responsibilities.

Inadequate funding is unquestionably a major impediment to the improvement of INS administration, but it is certainly not the only one. Closely related to the funding problem are the major changes that have occurred in the character of the enforcement effort as a result of the rapid rise in the number of aliens entering or seeking to enter the country and particularly the sharp increases in illegal immigration. These developments require a reevaluation of the entire immigration bureaucracy, the level of resources it requires, and the procedures that are most appropriate to carry out current and emerging administrative responsibilities. Such a rethinking is especially essential in light of the failure of the Simpson-Mazzoli bill since the immigration bureaucracy will have the sole burden of curtailing illegal immigration without the deterrence that the law would have provided.

5

Addressing the Administrative Problem

SUBSTANTIAL improvements in the administration of immigration policy could yield several important benefits. Greatly improved flow management, increased detection and expulsion of illegal immigration, and improved service to aliens who might otherwise slip into violation of immigration laws could substantially reduce illegal immigration and serve as a deterrent to those who might otherwise try to violate immigration laws. Such accomplishments could, in turn, alleviate the public's fears that the country is threatened by uncontrolled immigration and reduce the pressures for policies many consider onerous and detrimental to their civil rights. Finally, such improvements would appropriately reflect the continued importance of immigration to the society and constitute recognition that in an era of unprecedented mobility and unremitting pressures for admission to this country, immigration will continue to be immensely important.

In some respects the time is propitious for the federal government to substantially improve the administration of immigration policy. The severe problems that exist in every phase of the administration are now widely recognized by the public and policymakers. Failure by Congress to enact the Simpson-Mazzoli bill into law adds considerable urgency to

the need for such improvements since that measure might be
the only course open for curbing illegal immigration for a long
time.

Yet there are major obstacles to any decisive action on
administration. One is continued uncertainty about the kinds
of changes in immigration that are desired. Another is the cost
of making the needed improvements. A third is the failure of
policymakers and analysts to examine the full character and
dimensions of the changes that are required. Finally, it is by
no means clear how much can be achieved through improved
administration in view of the character of the migration phenomenon.

The Problem of Objectives and Priorities

Chapter 4 noted that the immigration bureaucracy is handicapped by the absence of clear, specific policy objectives and
that what appear to be administrative failures often are the
result of the failure of policymakers to make critical policy
choices. This problem complicates efforts to strengthen the
immigration bureaucracy. For example, although most people
want to curtail illegal immigration and would support improvements in the bureaucracy to accomplish this, other influential
groups want the labor force that illegal immigration provides
and are less eager for across-the-board improvements. Furthermore, the desire for improved administration often conflicts
with the public's strong humanitarian sentiments and with a
growing concern about impinging on the constitutional rights
of individuals regardless of their status.

The lengthy debate about the Simpson-Mazzoli bill exhibited
these conflicts. Most notable was the debate over the proposed
use of a reliable system for identifying all those eligible to work
as a component of the employer sanctions provision of the
law. The identification requirement was opposed on several

grounds, but most effectively on the ground that it would threaten individual freedom. It was dropped from the bill even though it clearly would have simplified enforcement of the employer sanctions. Similarly, the House voted to require that Immigration and Naturalization Service (INS) investigators obtain search warrants for open-field "raids" on illegal immigrants, thereby reversing a Supreme Court decision that such warrants were not essential. Here, too, proponents of the action invoked protection of individual rights in substantially adding to the difficulties INS investigators operate under. It is probably not coincidental that southwestern farmers found the increased difficulty for the INS highly beneficial.

Humanitarian concerns have been an equally strong constraint on administrative reforms. Much of that constraint was reflected in the attempts to deal with cases of "first asylum" claimants like the Mariel Bay Cubans, the Haitians, and even some Salvadorans and Nicaraguans. The arrival of these groups immediately created tensions between the sympathies of much of the public and the enforcement of existing laws. The tensions soon grew to embarrassment and anger as hundreds of these arrivals were detained in jail while the government tried to expel them or to adjudicate their claims. This problem is further complicated by the difficulties in determining who meets the qualifications for refugee status and by the very limited choices administrators have once such arrivals are judged ineligible for refugee status.

These problems indicate that the performance of the immigration bureaucracy and the prospects for improvement cannot be isolated from major policy reforms. Such reforms are needed to clarify the murky areas in current policies and practices and to provide new incentives for compliance, thereby easing the administrative burden. On the other hand, where such clarity and force are absent from public policy, a strong bureaucracy can help greatly in bringing order where chaos might otherwise prevail.

Paying for Improved Administration

There is widespread agreement among policymakers that inadequate funding is one of the most severe problems hampering effective administration of immigration policy. The need has been especially pronounced for the INS, where too few people with much too meager resources must cope with an increasingly demanding task of enforcing immigration laws in this country. Because the need for added resources has been so pronounced and so widely conceded by policymakers, it should be relatively easy to correct; increased appropriations need not raise the complex issues discussed earlier. In fact, both the House and Senate versions of the Simpson-Mazzoli bill addressed this need: the House bill authorized INS budget appropriations of $700 million and $715 million for fiscal years 1985 and 1986, substantial increases over 1984.[1]

This generous authorization by the House died with the Simpson-Mazzoli bill. Moreover, even though the House authorized the sharp increases in that bill, two weeks earlier it deleted a $20 million special increase in the INS budget recommended by the House Judiciary Committee to improve investigative and service operations. Thus, while Congress has readily acknowledged the need for added funds, it has been more reluctant to appropriate those funds.

Failure by Congress to appropriate the needed funds to strengthen administration of immigration policies appears to have been the result of (1) indecision about exactly what kinds of changes should be made; (2) the relatively low priority policymakers assign to immigration matters; and (3) ambivalence about curtailing illegal immigration. Although congressional committees have conducted extensive hearings on administrative problems and both Congress and the General Accounting Office have at various times urged substantially

---

1. *Congressional Record*, daily edition (June 13, 1984), pp. H5718–19.

increased expenditures for the INS, it is noteworthy that no comprehensive plans exist for improving the performance of the INS or the larger immigration bureaucracy.

Representative Edward R. Roybal, Democrat of California, offered an amendment to the Simpson-Mazzoli bill that is easily one of the most extensive proposals for administrative reform considered by the House.[2] That amendment called for the attorney general to develop within two months of enactment of the law specific plans for adequate Border Patrol activities, improved immigration and naturalization services, and enhanced community outreach activities. Moreover, that amendment, like most other proposed administrative reforms, seemed aimed at coping with the immediate burdens that would flow from enactment of the Simpson-Mazzoli bill.

Although Congress has seemed willing to support increased spending for administering immigration policy, there are real questions about how such sentiments would fare in the extremely difficult and competitive environment of an alarming budget deficit and intensive pressures for major reductions in federal government spending. Congressional action in slashing the INS appropriation for fiscal year 1985 as part of an across-the-board reduction in appropriations for the Departments of State and Justice suggests that even now such spending is not a very high priority. Moreover, a long-standing practice in Congress for undermining noble objectives has been to support the objectives but withhold or restrict the funds. That may very well have been at work in connection with improved administration of immigration policy.

The Scope of Reform

The measures contained in the unsuccessful Simpson-Mazzoli bill amount to an impressive array of actions to improve administration, yet it is unlikely that they would have been

2. Ibid., pp. H5716–17.

enough to ensure major improvements, especially if the requirements of the Simpson-Mazzoli bill are taken into account. Although the added funds would have allowed for substantially increased personnel and equipment, these additions would probably not have been adequate to cope with the massive new demands the bill would have imposed had it become law. The proposed amnesty, employer sanctions, and new adjudicative machinery all would have demanded considerable personnel and resources. Moreover, the amnesty might have stimulated others to attempt illegal entry in anticipation of another amnesty, thereby increasing the demands on Border Patrol and investigations personnel. The improvements might have done little more than to preserve the existing level and quality of administration.

Even putting aside the demands the bill would have imposed, the changes proposed would not have fundamentally altered the character of the bureaucracy or the quality of its performance, because they reflected too narrow a view of what reforms are needed. Congress gave virtually no attention to the structural and procedural problems that impair the performance of the bureaucracy, although approval of the limited reciprocal visa waiver was one significant change in procedure. Another was a proposal that surfaced in early Senate deliberations that called for local law enforcement officials to assist in some phases of enforcing immigration law. However, this idea, dubbed the "redneck special," was quickly abandoned, partly out of fear that local police, unfamiliar with immigration matters, might abuse this responsibility to the detriment of immigrants and some ethnic minorities.

Reform of the immigration bureaucracy must be comprehensive if it is to bring about significant improvement in the administration of immigration policy. It should go beyond the addition of personnel and equipment to the most severely strained areas of operation and should consider as well the need for changes in the structure of the bureaucracy and the allocation of responsibilities within it and changes in some procedures. Changes in bureaucratic structure and in the distribution of responsibilities appear promising, albeit controversial, ways to improve administration. Although they have not received a great deal of attention, a few studies have proposed changes worthy of consideration.

The boldest, and in many respects the most attractive, reorganization option that has been proposed is to combine the several agencies having enforcement responsibilities into a single new independent agency with complete responsibility for administering immigration policy. That step would do away with, or at least greatly reduce, the fragmented structure that now exists, improve communication and cooperation within the bureaucracy, and create a more prominent and presumably stronger entity capable of competing effectively for resources in the highly competitive federal budgetary process. Furthermore, it would dramatically underscore the importance of the enforcement responsibility within the federal government.

Such consolidation has been used successfully in other areas of government to improve the quality of policy enforcement. The Environmental Protection Agency (EPA), established in December 1970, is a case in point.[3] It was created by consolidating the tasks of eleven agencies that had environmental responsibilities. The objectives then were similar to those under consideration here, and some of them were achieved fairly quickly. With the creation of the EPA came a greatly increased federal commitment to environmental protection and a desire to increase the enforcement capacity of government. Of course, the reorganization has not solved all the problems encountered in enforcing environmental policy; some might argue that it merely created new problems. One difference between that case and the one being considered here, however, is that environmental problems generated considerable public support for stronger enforcement, something that is unlikely to emerge in the case of immigration.

Despite the likely benefits of consolidating all immigration enforcement responsibilities into a single agency, there are also

3. See Lynton K. Caldwell, *Man and His Environment: Policy and Administration* (Harper and Row, 1975), pp. 100–101.

strong arguments against it. Perhaps the most compelling is that the current distribution of responsibilities for enforcing immigration policy accurately reflects the character of immigration and the diverse interests it affects. Most noteworthy in this regard are the important foreign policy interests at stake that justify the extensive involvement of the State Department. Moreover, as a practical matter, some aspects of enforcement, such as visa issuance, clearly are more conveniently handled by the State Department than by any other agency. This is now the principal task of consular offices throughout the world and little would be gained by shifting responsibility for that activity elsewhere.

There have been occasional suggestions that responsibility for managing traffic across the land borders might be shifted from the INS to the Customs Bureau, which already is responsible for monitoring the flow of goods into the country. Some analysts have speculated that by combining those duties with those of the Border Patrol both might be performed better. However, it is not clear that a mere shift of the Border Patrol task elsewhere would ensure better performance of that task even if it improved the performance of the INS in other areas. The character of the land borders and the pattern of the traffic across them, especially the surreptitious crossings, would make the task equally demanding for another agency.

It appears that relatively modest structural adjustments might be more promising paths to improvement. For example, the status of the INS within the Justice Department might be elevated to enhance its visibility and voice in the federal bureaucracy. A permanent interagency unit linking the several segments of the immigration bureaucracy and other domestic agencies whose activities are closely connected to immigration might be mandated to better facilitate cooperation in administering immigration policy. Such a unit might include the Social Security Administration, the Bureau of Labor Standards, the Occupational Safety and Health Administration, and the Census Bureau, along with the agencies already having direct immigration responsibilities.

Finally, consideration might be given to increased cooperation between the INS and state and local law enforcement and social service agencies in enforcing immigration policies. Although the involvement of law enforcement officials unfamiliar with immigration laws poses risks of abuse and confusion, carefully delineated areas of collaboration could be an effective means of extending the reach of what will always be a small INS investigative force. Furthermore, such cooperation exists in virtually every other area of law enforcement. If violations of immigration laws are to be discouraged, such a broadened involvement across levels of government will be essential.

The changes in procedure are perhaps the most difficult to deal with. It is clear that INS investigative procedures like raids on gathering places and workplaces create considerable public ill will and raise difficult constitutional issues. Over the past decade some of these procedures have been modified in response to court decisions, thereby reducing the adverse reactions and the threats to individual rights. In other cases change is likely to come slowly in response to an evolving interpretation of what defines constitutionally protected rights. However, there are areas in which the INS can be urged to begin considering change.

One such area is the highly disruptive, sometimes dangerous practice of ad hoc raids on workplaces. Even though lawful when conducted with appropriate search warrants, it appears so inconsistent with the character of the U.S. society that it is almost certain to continue to arouse public antagonism and controversy. The alternatives to this procedure are not readily apparent and might be difficult to devise. However, they are worth pursuing. Moreover, with major improvements in other areas of enforcement the practice might become gradually unnecessary.

Prospects for Improving Administration

Many of the problems facing the immigration bureaucracy are common to all bureaucracies: demands far exceed the capacity to respond effectively; needs far exceed the financial resources provided to meet them; indecision or deliberate nondecisions create ambiguities with which bureaucrats must cope; and while the changing environment demands long-range planning, day-to-day challenges tend to make such planning very difficult, if not impossible.

In some respects, these widespread problems of bureaucracy are exaggerated in the immigration bureaucracy. Moreover, its own actions and capabilities are only part of the picture. Powerful forces beyond its control determine in large measure the degree and character of demands on it. Given these realities, it is unlikely that the immigration bureaucracy will be drastically improved in the near term. What is more likely is that persistent efforts will yield gradual improvements in the status quo or that a major development might force sweeping changes. After all, two massive waves of refugees, the Cubans and the Indochinese, forced the federal government to make extensive changes in the resettlement of refugees. A dangerous prospect is that such sweeping changes could reflect the country's fears rather than its generosity and thus lead to regressive reforms.

Barring such major developments, several relatively modest steps might now be taken in search of significant, though not dramatic, improvements. Those might well begin with actions to strengthen the INS and the Bureau of Consular Affairs and then proceed to broader reforms.

1. Drastically increase the size of the INS budget, not to carry out new responsibilities but to secure the people and equipment needed to much more effectively control illegal entries, apprehend and expel illegal immigrants, and improve its immigration-related services.

2. Speed up the planning and installation of automated data processing and storage systems to facilitate internal management, provide prompt and reliable service, and make reliable data available for public use.

3. Create a strong planning and research unit within the INS to help strengthen internal operations, respond effectively

to new developments, and play a more prominent role in developing immigration policies.

4. Examine the possibility of greatly increasing the presence of the Border Patrol in both fixed and mobile stations along the borders to reduce the incidence of surreptitious entries.

5. Establish a community outreach program along the lines proposed by Representative Roybal that would have as a principal mission educating the public about the activities of the INS and related immigration matters and serving as liaison between the public and the agency to better sensitize it to public attitudes toward various aspects of immigration law enforcement.

6. Build on the work already begun by the Office of Consular Affairs to develop and implement computer-assisted screening of visa applicants and machine-readable visas.

7. Establish a high-level task force to recommend improvements in the structure of the immigration bureaucracy and in the distribution of responsibility to facilitate increased communication, improve overall performance, and strengthen the profile of the immigration bureaucracy.

Index